"*Healing from Heaven* will astound you with its remarkable stories of emotional and physical healing through connection with those on the "other side." Dr. Daniel Ryan is a gifted healer and medium who takes the reader on a journey of self-discovery and transformation. This book will convince you that the soul never dies and lives on in all of us."

Susan Heim, Author and Editor for the best-selling
***Chicken Soup for the Soul* series**

"*Healing from Heaven* is for anyone who has grown to suspect that there is more to this existence than what meets the eye. Daniel's straightforward explanation of dimensions mystics have long understood, but scientists are only now beginning to detect, is an accessible, fascinating handbook to peeling back the layers of our loud world and experiencing our true delicate reality for yourself. The Healer's Guide to the Universe."

Mark DeCarlo, TV Host, Author, *A Fork on the Road*

"Daniel is a gifted seeker, healer, and writer. *Healing from Heaven* shares his journey into metaphysical realms and gives voice to the deeply healing power of our own sensitivity and creative awareness."

Chris Paine, Director, "Who Killed the Electric Car?"

"*Healing from Heaven* chronicles the incredible talent of Dr. Daniel Ryan as he reaches beyond the physical to help his clients heal from within. His intuitive abilities flow effortlessly in story after story, painting the picture of a true healer in every sense of the word."

Randy Rogers, Author
The Key of Life, A Metaphysical Investigation

"Twenty years ago I suffered with the idea that being incapacitated was never very far away. Then one day a friend said, "I've met a real healer, you should check him out."

Since I met Dan Ryan in 1991, I've been free of that idea and all that accompanied it. In addition, I've taken great pleasure in telling countless others about my friend, the "real healer." Every one undoubtedly feels the same sense of gratitude and wonder that I do. Not to mention the elation of being healed."

Patrick Leonard, Music Producer, (Madonna, Jewel, Elton John, Pink Floyd, Bon Jovi, Michael Jackson)

"Dr. Daniel Ryan, through his teaching and practice, gives insight into how he came to recognize his gifts and now shares them with us. As a western trained physician, I am acutely aware of the limitations embedded in western medicine. Dr. Ryan, a modern day Avatar, blends the world of traditional medicine and eastern philosophy to create a universal love and spiritual healing that we have been craving. Thank you, Dr Ryan, for sharing this incredible gift!

James Peace, M.D.
Physician, Surgeon, Clinical Researcher

Healing from Heaven

A Healer's Guide to the Universe

Daniel Ryan, D.C.

Transformation Media Books

Transformation Media Books

Published by Transformation Media Books, USA
www.TransformationMediaBooks.com

An imprint of Pen & Publish, Inc.
Bloomington, Indiana
(812) 837-9226
info@PenandPublish.com
www.PenandPublish.com

Cover photo ℅ istockphoto.com/Eraxion
Cover photo: www.comstock.com
Cover design and text layout by Jane Hagaman

ISBN: 978-0-9845751-0-7
Library of Congress Control Number: 2010929896

This book is printed on acid free paper.

Printed in the USA

Dedication

This book is dedicated to the foundation of unwavering love and support of Nicole my wife and sojourn partner;

to my parents Robert and Diane Ryan, for their example that love and commitment perseveres even in adversity;

and to my beloved brilliant and joyful children, Jhade and Grace. My love for them is reason to exist.

Contents

Foreword

You could say I was skeptical. Dubious. And in Dr. Daniel Ryan's case, it was a double dose. As a child of a generation that was dubious about the efficacy of chiropractors when compared to more conventional forms of medicine, Dr. Ryan's healing power reshaped my entire way of thinking and has been treating my family and me for many years now. However, it was how I experienced him on a number of occasions separate from his role as a Doctor of Chiropractic, that I previously didn't believe in, that altered my way of thinking about life in general.

Comedy is the field I toil in. I'm a writer by trade. I put words in an order with every hope that they hold your interest and make you laugh when spoken or read. It's a space I'm comfortable in. Drama is outside of my wheelhouse. Mysteries confound me. And the paranormal is something I never took seriously. Communicating with people who've passed? Courtesy of a spiritual medium? At most, it was merely a romantic wish as portrayed by Whoopi Goldberg's character in the movie *Ghost*. But that began to change the day a family member came back from a session with Dan Ryan and told me that when he was working with her a recently deceased friend of hers made his presence known through Dr. Ryan; who began speaking in the friend's jargon and had information he couldn't possibly have gotten through any other source.

Subsequently, I had a similar experience when a beloved grandmother spoke through Dr. Ryan and offered me characteristically sage advice at a time of personal crisis. Soon after, I passed the word along to a number of friends (who were equally cynical about such things) who reported that they, too, reconnected with loved ones. They not only gained a sense of closure but were now subscribing to the comforting belief that the word 'death' is a misnomer—as life does indeed continue elsewhere when these bodies that house us can no longer do their jobs.

This book describes many instances where Dr. Ryan—a spiritual man, doctor, husband, parent and dog owner—ventures beyond our tangible realm to communicate with those who have crossed over to bring closure and healing to those that remain in this dimension.

And while reading these stories, you will get to know the man I know. The man who has the ability to venture beyond the limitations of the finite mind and the illusion of its security and structure. A man who, in his unwavering commitment to the betterment of others, ushers in a reality beyond your identity, beyond this dimension. An extraordinary man whose only discernible fault, should you ever visit him in his Los Angeles office, is that he does not validate for parking.

Alan Zweibel
New York City, 2011

An original *Saturday Night Live* writer, Alan Zweibel has won multiple Emmy and Writers Guild awards for his work in TV which also includes *It's Garry Shadling's Show* and *Curb Your Enthusiasm.* He collaborated with Billy Crystal on the Tony award winning play *700 Sundays* and his novel, *The Other Shulman* won the 2006 Thurber Prize for American Humor. His newest novel, written with Dave Barry, is *Lunatics* (Putnam, January, 2012).

Introduction

This is about a journey of the heart. Your journey will be different from mine, and from the others that you read about in this book. But these experiences serve as inspiration and a catalyst to reveal your own divinity, and provide you with the tools to reconnect and sustain your connection with Spirit. Through others' examples, exercises and visioning guidance on the following pages, you can learn to overcome spiritual and energetic blockages to activate and realize authentic freedom.

I address some of the most fundamental challenges of healing, connecting and maintaining the connection with Spirit. As we move along the path of spiritual evolution, Spirit inspires us from exactly where we are, not waiting until we reach some exalted hypothetical state of "enlightenment," for that is already inherent in our nature. We live in an incredibly kind universe, yearning at our beck and call to support us in our endeavor of "self-realization." It isn't accomplished, but merely realized.

In my humble and modest beginnings, I was completely unaware of my innate potential and the magnificence that we all possess. Much of my attention was based on basic survival and, oftentimes, one day at a time. Although many aspects of my journey were difficult, I can say now with the utmost sincerity that it was all a perfect catalyst for my particular soul's yearning to express more of itself—and the same holds true for many others with whom I have worked.

Remarkable brilliance and infinite potential are our birthright. That is to say this is not another self-help book that will show you how to apply a formula to be happy or promise that this is the "true" way to enlightenment. Rather, it is an example of how we are all unique, and it will encourage you to find your own way to reconnect with Spirit.

Beyond words, this book holds the frequency and vibration of a soul's heartfelt voyage toward peace—peace of mind and heart, and the joy that is released as a result of aligning oneself with the pure, unadulterated desire of our souls, to express the love and inclusiveness that are inherent in our nature. It is my intention not only to convey a transmission of healing frequency unbound by the physical laws of the finite realm, but also to encourage you to trust your intuition to provide a vehicle for transformation, to see and act upon the potential that is already within you.

It doesn't matter who you think you are, or what you believe your limitations to be. By surrendering and opening to the one power, the vitality, passion and creative beauty yearning to be expressed through you will surface. Merely beginning with the faith of a mustard seed, you will begin to see a demonstration of this manifest in your life.

About the Stories

This book is not only for healers, it's for anyone who wishes to connect with or has a curiosity for the spiritual realm or spiritual awakening. This message is beyond a specific religion, culture or race. It is all-inclusive, as we all have the capacity to become self-realized. Through my experiences in working with thousands of individuals, I have guided many people to expedite their own opening to connect with Spirit and change their lives.

In some chapters, I describe my personal journey to recognizing my soul's purpose. In other chapters, I write about my experiences with others' healing journeys and reconnecting with loved ones. Finally, near the end of the book, a guide to help you overcome barriers and activate your own untapped potential is provided. Feel free to refer to the final section for a greater understanding of certain aspects of stories while navigating your way through the chapters.

For clarification, although I have a professional education as a doctor of chiropractic, my role as a chiropractor working with patients is totally separate and independent of my role as a medium and energy healer. The principles of medium and energy healing do not require any specific diagnosis, nor is there any particular condition or disease which is treated. The statements, experiences and opinions in this book are not intended to diagnose, treat, cure, or prevent any disease. Also, please note that the names and locations in this book are fictitious.

Throughout this book, I use the interchangeable terms of Spirit, Love, God, Universal Intelligence, One Mind, Source, and Authentic Self to interweave the interconnectedness of all things. I have chosen stories that may resonate with a greater audience.

Daniel Ryan, D.C.
Los Angeles, 2011

PART I

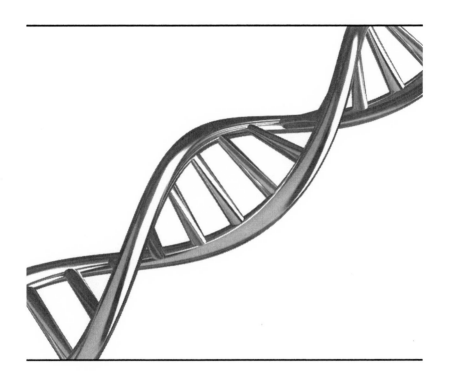

MY STORY

Chapter 1

Evolution of a Medium

Whatever you can do, or dream you can, begin it.
Boldness has genius, power, and magic in it.

—Johann Wolfgang von Goethe

The strong pungent smell of tanbark stirred my senses. As
if waking from a lucid dream I moved my head slightly from
the side, the bark pricked the back of my head. A euphoric
sensation of increased circulation and neurological stimula-
tion tingled through my supine body. My head was hot and it
pulsed loudly. Utterly unaware of how long my eyes had been
open, the black dissipated and they came into focus. The sun
high in the bright blue sky, shaded slightly with white billowy
clouds, pierced my consciousness.

The teacher appeared in my field of vision with a look of
serious concern after hearing the account from my friend Billy.
"We were swinging from the bars up high and he fell and his
head hit that bar on the bottom," he said. Recess was over and
time to get back to our first grade classroom. When the teacher
asked how I was doing, "I'm okay," stammered out. Dazed and
head pounding, I attempted to shake it off. An hour later the
janitor discovered me sitting on the concrete walkway outside
the classroom, my head leaning back against the cool stucco

wall. "I'm on my way to the drinking fountain, I'm thirsty," I said almost as a question. Apparently, I wasn't okay and upon further questioning I had no recollection of how I got there.

My mother picked me up early from school. By late afternoon there was a lump the size of a baseball protruding from the top of my forehead, I was despondent. Next thing I remember was a bright piercing light being shone into my right eye that woke me. Utterly unalarmed by the doctor or hospital room, that is until I witnessed the grave concern on my mothers face. Due to the severity of the frontal bone fracture, a neurosurgeon was standing by for seventy-two hours in case they needed to open the cranium to release the increasing pressure of the swelling, a critical life or death situation.

Over these three days, as I faded in and out of consciousness, I had snapshot memories, a needle in my arm, a tightening blood pressure cuff around my arm, a kind nurse searching beyond my response to her question of "how are you feeling Danny?" To my fascination, at one point I found myself looking down at my body with wires attached to my head. It was oddly peaceful from this expansive, light and serenely hazy place. I seemed to be floating away and perfectly okay with it when suddenly as if all the air had been vacuumed out of the room, I was thrust back into my body. Fear gripped me with a cold sweat cooling my skin. My scalp hurt where the wires were attached. Stunned by how small I now felt, out of nowhere, a peaceful, loving, tingling feeling held me. I couldn't see anyone, but I felt the presence very clearly. I was startled by the immediate contrast of emotion. This presence reassured me that everything would be okay and that I would always be safe. This was the first time in my life that I felt such a deep peace in my heart, as if I were connected to everything. Fortunately the swelling stayed in check and I had a remarkable recovery without the need for surgery, even though I had to wear a football helmet to school for three weeks, "just in case."

This was my first conscious recollection of what I now recognize as my connection with Spirit. As I struggled with challenges in life over the years, I would always remember this connection and call upon it for strength, it had permanently forged a knowing of a power greater than self in my consciousness. After that experience I no longer felt as confined to my physical body and maintained a sense our expansive nature.

As a child, sometimes I felt like a freak. I would see dancing, twinkling lights and waves of energy before me that would warp my field of vision like heat does in the desert. I would see a cloud of energy around a person that felt happy, sad or angry. I remember seeing a man on the street, and I instantly felt sad and defeated. His head was down and shoulders rounded. He had a female spirit next to him. She was trying to get through to him. It was as if she was yelling at him, but he couldn't hear her. Another time, I saw a woman in a restaurant with all these babies around her energetically. I felt so happy and optimistic. I later found out that she was a neonatal nurse at the children's hospital. It was a constant challenge for me to simply function day to day without getting knocked sideways by other people's emotions. My earliest memories were filled with visions and feelings that made it very difficult to cope with this reality at times. I learned to keep this a secret because when I tried to explain rarely did anyone understand. Even though I have never been afraid of the spiritual dimension, the dramatic swings of what I was feeling that had me question my sanity at times. Actually, in retrospect, I realize that interacting with the spiritual dimension always made much more sense to me than the subconscious mixed messages I received from others.

When I gazed upward at the three white crosses in front of my church, I noticed they formed a perfect triangle. They reached for the sky ten stories high as if they were ascending to the heavens. Navigating my way through the paradoxes of my particularly religious upbringing, I attempted to integrate my secular view into this world, but it didn't always fit.

The youth group at my church provided a safe haven, filled with direction for morals and character. It built a foundation for me to rely upon in my times of confusion. It also kept me off the street where I could get into trouble, as I was known to be a "very active child." The crowd I was hanging out with at the time was up to a lot of mischief and on the verge of getting into serious trouble that could mark us for life. Their misdemeanors of vandalism, disturbing the peace, and malicious mischief would be the precursors to felony offenses that many of them later committed.

Fortunately, I saw a vision of two completely different paths I could take: one that would continue to lead me down a path of destruction, and another that would be a positive life full of love and fulfillment. I yearned for the latter, but I couldn't conceive of how I could achieve it. It was my dream, and I reached for it by having faith that my direction was correct. I can see now that Spirit was giving me a bird's eye view of my choices and showing me that it was within my power to make either one my reality. But there were still pieces missing from my puzzle and, from an early age, I felt extremely confined by the dogma of my religious community. It seemed to me that it wasn't the whole picture.

As far back as I can remember, I had been trying to decipher what I was feeling in the world. As a child, while in the presence of others, I became accustomed to intuitively assessing the energetic environment, although I didn't realize at the time that I was tapping into what they were feeling. Not until I grew older did I learn that all the different feelings I had were not all mine.

Many years passed before I would fully understand that the swings I experienced were a combination of feeling others' emotions, my own skeletons beckoning emancipation, and spirits attempting to communicate with me, at times all at once. This led me on a journey of discovery, the impetus being simply my desire for peace of mind. Acutely aware of my insidious and repetitious thoughts, I sought out answers to quiet the madness. First, I turned to what I had known: prayer, the Bible, and communion with silence. I also became fascinated with spiritual psychology and development books. I learned about world religions, mystics and self-realization.

But where did the intuitive realm and psychic phenomena fit in? Well, it didn't, not in my family anyway. It was considered flat-out evil, and if you were open to it, you would be exposing yourself to darkness and, most certainly, be possessed by the devil. The stigma my family placed on the spiritual realm created a substantial conflict for me. I became acutely aware of the fact that some of the things that I saw and felt challenged my existing belief systems.

Later, as a man in my late thirties, my mother revealed to me in a conversation that she had spirits come and speak to her from time to time, including the spirit of my grandmother. When I asked her why she never spoke of this before, she simply said, "Oh, you can't talk about that or people will think you're crazy."

She also said that she had known I was a "healer" since I was a baby. My mother was extremely intuitive, but she rarely talked about it. But it was our conversations that finally helped make sense of all of the confusion. It was my mother who provided a foundation of unconditional love that helped me evolve and understand my gift. In the end, I came to the conclusion that I needed to be true to my intuitive direction above all else.

But these and other questions took backstage to a much more critical issue during my childhood; my safety. There was another reason I became highly adept at assessing energetic environments. How could I be safe at home on Friday or Saturday night with a raging alcoholic father wrecking havoc around the house? It was a family secret that he was able to hide as he taught my Sunday school class. My father's contradictory lifestyle catalyzed my arduous journey of uncovering my abilities. This also provided me a perfect environment to develop my sensitivity. It was a matter of necessity for me as he released these negative emotional energetic patterns, so I learned through experience.

One early October morning, close to 2 a.m., a low rumble of arguing voices filtered through my bedroom walls. I was six years old, and it had been another out-of-control Friday night, which I hoped had been put to rest as the house quieted down. Suddenly, I jumped up to the sound of my bedroom door swinging open and my mother yelling, "Let's go, Danny! We need to find your father." She yanked me out of bed, and we raced to the door and out into the night together. In our station wagon, we sped away through the darkness in search of my father. After several minutes, we came to an abrupt stop in front of a bar. The light from the bar's illuminated red sign filled up the car and accentuated the anger in my mother's face as she pulled me outside.

I held on in stride, my six-year-old self desperately wanting to be there to protect my mother. She swung open the heavy wooden door with such fury that it rattled the wine and pilsner glasses suspended meticulously above the bar. A whoosh of damp, musky, alcohol-tinged air slapped my face as we crossed the threshold of the establishment.

I gazed down at my mother's white nursing shoes that she had polished so many times. They had served her so well during all those years of service. I watched as they marched forward into the bar late that night, void of fear. It seemed almost blasphemous for her to be wearing those shoes here in this dark place, where souls were lost on the rocks.

A tightness gripped my chest as my mom let out a stifling, high-pitched shrill, "YOU SON OF A *&^%$@#$!" People in the bar ducked, as if a gun had just been fired over their heads. She pulled me forward quickly, and a button popped off my pajamas. My cuff was sealed within the clasp of her tight grip around my hand.

The bar with the large mirror behind it read, "JACK DANIELS." I was pleased with myself that I could read it since I was only in the first grade. Must be the owner's name, I thought.

My mother's voice cleared our path, which ended at the bar stool where my dad sat. Her wave of anger broke through his calm exterior, nearly knocking him off the barstool. "I'VE HAD IT, YOU SON OF A *#%^&*&." My father grabbed the bar for balance, his stool now balancing on two legs.

My mother rarely ever swore, and if she did, it meant you were in the worst kind of trouble. My father's face reflected shock at my mother's string of cursing. We stopped one step short of my father, and my mother doused his face with his drink. This was the exclamation point that punctuated her statement. Immediately, we did an about-face, heading straight back to our 1964 Ford Country Squire station wagon. I exited in slow motion as my eyes met those of the bartender behind the bar. His eyes were filled with tears. I felt nothing except cold in the autumn night air.

On the other side of the doorway sat our tan station wagon, with the faux wood paneling. The doors had been left open, the engine still running. The light from across the street illuminated the exhaust from the muffler. It had been raining, and a car swooshed by just then in the wetness. I wasn't sure if my mother's face was wet from the rain or from tears. I didn't ask.

On the way home, my mother's trembling voice finally broke the silence. "I'm sorry, Danny."

"Is Dad coming home?" I asked.

"Yes, he'll be home in a little while," she answered, not doing a very good job of hiding her disdain for him.

There was an uncomfortable silence at our house over the next week that eventually got swallowed up. The other coping mechanism of our household—laughter—didn't surface this time. The responsibilities of managing a household with four kids under the age of ten, two still in diapers, ensued. I realized I needed to fend for myself. As a survival mechanism more than anything else, I learned to trust only what was in alignment with my heart. This gut feeling guided me forward in spite of fear.

My dad used to say, "You'll understand when you have kids." My parents were completely committed to the selfless service of raising a large family while facing their own skeletons. My dad's old-fashioned method of discipline inflicted more pain emotionally than it ever did physically. As an adult, I respect and appreciate my father in a much more inclusive, accepting way. And he was right: having kids of my own definitely enlightened my perspective!

Chapter 2

Breaking Open

*Imagination is more important
than knowledge. For knowledge is limited,
whereas imagination embraces
the entire world, stimulating progress,
giving birth to evolution.*

—*Albert Einstein*

As an adult, I accepted my life's calling, and I made a commitment to use my intuitive abilities to help others heal. I became interested in helping people fulfill their innate potential by healing the whole person through the physical, spiritual, mental, emotional and ethereal levels. I allowed myself to be guided by intuition and divine intervention. The latter became the catalyst for what I would become.

Having a taste of Spirit only increased my appetite for the divine. My imagination opened the door to this world, and as I grew into adulthood, my intuition became a vehicle for transformation. As my interest in the spirit world grew, moments of self-realization came to me as Zen experiences. The universal mind had always been expressing itself through me, but I only became aware of it incrementally. There was a log rhythmic effect happening as my interest grew, as if I were waking up from a dream and guided by an invisible force. During the process, I was in a state of "no mind," with the universal energy from the infinite realm streaming in the now. I was letting go and learning to trust, to have faith in my intuitive direction, which guided me to let go even further.

Once, I told a friend that you didn't need to go to India to have a spiritual experience, but when my church announced a trip to India, I wanted to experience this kind of spiritual expansion as well. This was not the church from my youth, but one called Agape International, facilitated by Reverend Michael Bernard Beckwith and his wife, Ricky Byers Beckwith. As soon as I heard about the trip, I knew I had to go. I was ready to see it all; I was ready for India.

When you have the intention to open and reveal the depth of your soul's vastness, the universe conspires in your favor to bring you into alignment with your soul's desire for expression. As we take one step toward our divinity, the universe responds tenfold in our favor. Before my trip, I entered the following message from Spirit into my journal:

> *Eyes pierce the veil in the absence of fear.*
> *Feel the earth between your toes daily to allow your mother to*
> *   embrace you.*
> *As your heart breaks open, allow your joyous tears to quench*
> *   your newfound thirst.*
> *And when the breeze of Spirit kisses your face so dear, know*
> *   India's sweet nectar is here.*

My trip to India shattered some of my belief systems. People say that you don't vacation in India, you experience it. Believe them. During my trip, I set my intention to the universe to see the world anew, to jump off the cliff with reckless abandon, free of all the constraints and limitations of this world. I wanted to experience pure intimacy and fearless love in all my relationships. I was mentally ready and spiritually prime for India. Before I knew it, I found myself at the airport ready to board a flight to Delhi with a small group of spiritual seekers.

Reverend Michael, as he was affectionately known, had been one of my spiritual mentors for years. For those who know of him, he is a great visionary and mystic, and for those who know him personally, he is a compassionate, kind, loving soul as well. I had decided to eat only vegetarian on this trip, do yoga for an hour a day, and mediate for an hour, morning and night. I did everything that I could to be completely present during the trip. I wanted answers to everything.

My prayer and intention to the universe was that I was ready to see it all. I was ready to trust that the universe would work in my favor to fulfill my greatest potential in this incarnation. If you have similar intentions in any way, shape or form, put on your seatbelt because your wish will be granted. But be aware of one caveat: your "life" as you currently know it may blow up and turn inside out in the process.

I was now a Doctor of Chiropractic, and the thought of potentially being exposed to malaria, yellow fever, typhoid or all the other diseases in this exotic Petri dish proved to be extremely unsettling. Was I over-informed? Or did I just need to trust? The answer turned out to be both.

Leaving the airport terminal in Delhi, the pungent air repelled me slightly. I felt as if I were in the middle of a *National Geographic* documentary as I stepped into this ancient, mystical country. Upon leaving the main terminal, throngs of people in a sea of brightly colored saris desperately reached out to us from the railed-off walkway. We were quickly identified by our guides and ushered onto what looked like a 1970s transit bus.

As we turned left onto the main thoroughfare, a man lay motionless in the middle of the street, with a motorcycle toppled over beside him. The traffic continued indifferently, navigating around him. Swarms of motorcycles, bicycles, small cars, and various other unrecognizable forms of transportation ebbed and flowed within inches of one another. This was my introduction to the vast difference between personal space in America and personal space in India.

Later, we arrived at our five-star hotel (equivalent to a three-star hotel in America). After our long journey, I decided to go for a run through the streets of New Delhi. It became uncomfortably obvious how isolated my life had been until then. The moment I emerged from the hotel, I witnessed the hopelessness of a shoeless boy, standing atop a pile of waste and begging. The stark contrast to my American life became the melody of the emotional swing I would hear throughout India. Desperately attempting to maintain my false sense of sterility and safety, I had yet to "arrive" in India. Back at the hotel, I blew my nose, and black soot filled the tissue. India has a way of expediting catharsis by assaulting the senses, but I was up for the challenge.

That evening, a few of us ventured out to an ancient Hindu temple where the priest performed prayers and *darshan* (Sanskrit for "sight or beholding"). As I entered, a petite Indian man placed his thumb to my forehead, leaving a red dot the size of a nickel, which signified I had attended services. I listened and swayed with the crowd in the small 300-year-old temple. The priest sang his Hindu prayers, and while I didn't understand what I was hearing, something about them still moved me. It was magical, and I could feel myself letting go, the power of the sacred hymn disintegrating my barriers. It didn't even bother me now that my personal space no longer existed. My space within had expanded.

Humming along in the bliss of the moment, I heard the words of the hymn leave my mouth in Hindi. Tears rolled down my face, and the pulse of the melody swayed my body, free in the beauty of it all. After a few moments, my logical mind slapped my face, protesting, "You don't know Hindi!" My body froze. I took a quick inhale. "Okay, relax! You're just experiencing something different. Go with it," I told myself.

It was too late. My mind had taken me hostage once again. But I knew that this was my process of unfolding. When I left the temple that evening, my soul naked to the world, the heart of India flowed right through me. My vision extended beyond the poverty, disease, and filth of the land, and it all felt so beautiful. That was the moment I arrived in India.

In the ensuing days, we traveled through Northern India, eventually arriving in Katmandu, Nepal. There, our group met with another small affiliate church group to share experiences. We paired off around the room, and a woman sat across from me on the floor, cross-legged. Our eyes locked. She described a table she had seen that day in the bazaar with intricately placed mosaic tiles on the top. She had been so moved by it that she was thinking about having it shipped home from Varanasi, India, the holy city. This was day twelve of our two-week journey through Northern India and Nepal, meditating, practicing daily yoga, praying and chanting throughout sacred temples. The fruits of my intention were about to be revealed.

Immersed in the moment, I listened intensely, and my mind

was completely still. As I watched the woman's face, it suddenly disappeared. It was all I could do not to jump out of my skin. A tsunami of emotion washed away what I thought I knew. I shuddered and sobbed, as a river of joy emanated from my core, shattering many limited belief systems on its way. I witnessed a transcendental beauty that I had never known; a veil lifted, revealing the infinite vastness of all things where her face had been. I continued staring in amazement into this infinite realm. Then, out of nowhere, my face appeared where her face had been. My body began an involuntary sobbing of elation. I became weightless, and time expanded somehow. When it was my turn to share, all I said was, "There is nothing to say," as the tears of joy fell from my chin.

Our group of thirty people then gathered to make an inner circle and an outer circle as we rotated around, greeting one another. What I saw was a beauty beyond human understanding: I could not see anyone in the room as separate from me any more than my own hands or feet. This was a feeling of total oneness with all people, places, and things. All feelings of competition, accumulation, and separation seemed ludicrous and left me immediately.

After a few weeks in India, I came to expect the unexpected, and I looked for miracles everywhere I went. I stopped defining them, and my "little self" dissolved in the vast sea of energy. All people, places, and things became the flow. I witnessed them more, everywhere I looked. I had entered the fourth dimension.

Chapter 3

Oneness

*Your work is to discover your work
and then with all your heart to give yourself to it.*

—*Buddha*

In India, I learned that a vital component in breaking through belief systems is addressing the obstacles that you must overcome when communicating with other dimensions. First and foremost among these obstacles is *intention.* Intention must be crystal clear. Spirit has a way of opening us up from where we are, and you may find that your desires change as you expand in consciousness. We manifest our own reality. In other words, if you want to know what you believe, look at your life.

Initially, this may sound a bit callous, but to truly be empowered and step into your infinite potential, it is imperative to be bold and set fire to your imagination, to allow your soul's desires to come forth. It is futile to focus on what you already see manifested and attempt to change it because you will simply manifest more of the same. Changes will only come to fruition if you hold the feeling of that which you *desire.* For example, when you have the experience of a feeling, such as being in love, you can access that feeling in your being and let yourself continue to feel it regardless of whether you are

currently in love or not. By holding this feeling in your imagination, you bring your energy into alignment with that which
you desire to create in your life. The biggest problem is that
you may not realize how powerful you are. This is why it is
important to be aware of what you believe and what you think,
because you will create what you believe.

Our creativity and imagination come through the same
Source. Therefore, it is important to allow our imaginations to
be vehicles for seeing our potential. The soul is always seeking
to express itself, and reaching your potential is a matter of
learning how to listen. You need to believe it before you see it,
not see it and you'll believe it. Where your attention and intention are ultimately will be what you manifest in your life.

The fact is that we are always manifesting, whether it is conscious or unconscious. We are pleased when we see that our
dreams are coming true, but disillusioned and confused when
undesirable qualities appear in our lives. An illuminated or
self-realized being is someone who is manifesting from the
here and now, completely conscious of the choices he or she
is making.

This is done by illuminating outdated belief systems and
becoming a clear channel to facilitate change. We don't need to
acquire anything; we just need to get out of the way and let our
Authentic Self come forth. Stagnant energetic patterns in the
physical body that correlate with fixed belief systems can manifest
unwanted results in your life and give the sensation of being
"stuck" or in an "endless karmic loop." One definition of insanity is repeating the same actions but expecting different results.

By clearing out stagnant belief systems and aligning yourself with your soul's desires, you can create consciously and
realize your true potential. This becomes a vehicle for a cathartic transformation to authentic empowerment and happiness
that is unrelated to external circumstance. It is extremely difficult to communicate with other dimensions and realize your
full potential when you have the constant distraction of incessant unconscious patterns plaguing you. (I explain in greater
detail how to eradicate these patterns in a later chapter, "Healing the Healer.")

Beware of the mind's incessant dialogue that says, "Others
may do this, but I can't," or "It's impossible." This is an attempt

by the rigid ego structure to perpetuate a sense of separation derived from its fear of annihilation. Breaking free from the shackles and limitations of the ego, and realizing that you are an expansive soul having a human experience, will bring about the liberation of your soul.

We are all candidates for awakening. By answering the call of Spirit, we can all actively participate in the co-creative process of developing an enlightened society. Recognizing and developing our particular talents and skills and sharing them will benefit the whole. This is not done by allowing external circumstances to dictate our direction unconsciously, but by having a clear intention to wake up through devotion, meditation, prayer, intention and divine intuitive inspiration received as we allow Spirit to guide us. Acting upon our guidance is essential to complete our participation in human evolution.

The Light

Infused with light
A shadow's flight
The night beckons
But the day has arrived
Sublime surrender its tender touch
Yes, I remember we can't love too much
A smile opens the door inward
The exhilaration of feeling alive
I lay down my cloak and dagger
I see they have only made me stagger
For I have found the greatest weapon of all
The rapture of the innocent call
For this I am a believer
I am love
The great reveler

—Daniel Ryan

PART II

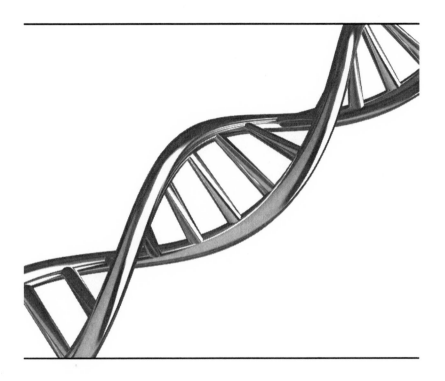

OTHERS' STORIES

Chapter 4

Gratitude

Gratitude is the prayer of the enlightened.

—*Daniel Ryan*

Spirit has a way of guiding us to an awareness of our innate magnificence that is waiting to be realized. As we become more aware of the vastness of our being, a quickening happens. Choices are more obvious, negative or addictive habits are less interesting, and our attention shifts, which alters our perception of reality, as we have known it. This new reality comes with the gratitude of appreciating the miracles that are ever present all around us, and that we may have taken for granted previously. The sun rises and warms the earth. Photosynthesis provides food and converts carbon dioxide to oxygen. Physiologically, the body converts oxygen and food to create energy via a chemical reaction, releasing CO_2 as one of the byproducts completing the cycle—one of an infinite number of miracles occurring constantly. When we focus on the incredible things that are happening all the time, it raises our vibration. By raising our vibration, we are able to experience a knowing of the great synchronicity of life, a knowing that surpasses human logical understanding. Hence, that person you may call a fool wearing a huge smile with an eternal sparkle in his eyes knows a secret. Gratitude is the prayer of the enlightened.

Mind Reader

Early on as I began working with many people, I had the unique opportunity to hone my intuitive skills. A friend of mine, Virginia, who worked as an energetic body healer, strongly encouraged me to "play with the energy" to see what I could feel. During a session with Virginia, I placed my hands about six inches above her to see if I could feel anything. I moved them around, and I felt a distinct border to an energy field.

As I continued with my eyes closed, I saw a man in a dark cloak and large black-brimmed hat come forth and continue past. My attention went to a river over which a golden ball of light was suspended. I felt an urgency to help release this light. As I helped free this golden ball of energy, it moved up and away, and for some reason I didn't want it to go. The ball of light then said to me, "It's okay. It can happen that fast."

This whole process took about two minutes as I stood next to Virginia, supine on the table. I opened my eyes and asked Virginia how she was doing.

She opened her eyes and asked me, "How are *you* doing? You look like you just saw a ghost."

"Well, tell me, did you see or feel anything?" I asked.

"Yes, I saw this beautiful ball of golden light rise up and hover over me for a while before it went up and away."

Saying that I was intrigued would be an understatement. I'm still not sure about the true meaning of that incident, but I'm sure it was some kind of lesson to help dissolve barriers. I understand now that Virginia came to help nudge me along in my development. I started consciously tuning into the energy of my clients and within a couple of weeks, six different spirits came to me in one day to convey messages to clients. I had always felt them around and felt people empathically since childhood, but now I began to intentionally focus my attention to try to make sense of it all. I was having a blast, fascinated by this vast sea of pliable energy. On some level, I believed I would never know exactly what it all meant until the following realization that it was real slapped me in the face.

The Brother

The first time I saw Sari, she reminded me of a little wounded bird trying to find her way out of a cage. We met in a class that focused on deepening one's connection to Spirit. After the lecture, we would separate into smaller groups of five or six, including the facilitator. In this intimate setting, it was safe to see and be seen. I instantly felt connected to Sari, and I wanted to help her heal. We became fast friends and worked on some projects together for class. She eventually came to me for help. As we began a session together, her tears washed away her story of emotional abuse that had festered deep within her being since early childhood. According to Sari's analysis of her own psyche, she never received the validation from her parents that she needed to form a solid self-esteem. Sari felt compelled to continue her journey of self-discovery to better her life experience. Our mutual trust served as a catalyst for what was about to happen.

A few minutes into our session, the back of my neck began to tingle. This was a familiar tantalizing sensation that alerts me to the presence of a spirit. I began to see the image of a small man. Everything about his head and face was round, the kind of roundness that is the result of a lifetime of giving and the blessing that is received through selflessness. His warm voice poured into me like hot tea, loosening my shoulders instantly. He said his name was Heimy, and that he was Sari's maternal grandfather. I enjoyed his presence. It was comforting, like a smile from an old friend. I answered him telepathically with a question.

"What kind of name is Heimy anyway?" I had never heard this name before. I thought it seemed odd. If I was going to let his presence be known, I wanted to be sure that I had it right. Apparently, it was an eastern European name, more common to his generation. He insisted that I heard him correctly, and wanted me to let Sari know that he was here to talk to her.

"Does your grandfather's name begin with an H?" I asked.

"No," she said, "both of my grandfathers' names began with J."

"Well, this spirit is telling me his name is Hei-my."

"Oh, yes, Heimy, that's my great-grandfather's name. Actually, I didn't know him that well," Sari explained. Later, she discovered from her mother that Heimy actually was her grandfather's name, not her great-grandfather's.

"He would like to talk to you about your family. Is that okay with you?"

"Yes, of course."

"You will be the catalyst to change your family matrix and the inspiration to help expand their consciousness," Heimy said.

Sari looked exasperated as she pleaded, "Do I need to move back home to do it?"

Heimy laughed, and then confidently replied, "It's not what you do physically, so much as the energetic shift that you make internally."

Heimy's laughter eased the tension, and as he relaxed, it became easier to understand him. In my experience, there's a learning curve for spirits to communicate as well, for they need to slow down their vibration just as I need to speed up my vibration to meet in the middle, almost like tuning in a radio. If forced by either party, it decreases the quality or breaks the connection.

Heimy continued, "Having the intention put into action is important, although, ultimately, your action needs to be in alignment with your soul's intention for unity for it to be effective."

Heimy showed me a small, curly-haired black and white terrier. He said that her mom really loved her dog.

"Oh, that's Jessie he's talking about, my mom's dog. He just recently passed. That's incredible. Do you see him?"

"Yes, Jessie is there with Heimy, and he wants you to let your mom know that he is being well cared for. Your mother was devastated when Jessie died."

"Yes, she was," Sari sighed.

Heimy continued, "You may not know this, but your mother has been suicidal many times throughout her life."

Sari's shoulders reached for her ears, and the tears began to flow down the temporary furrows the pain had sculpted in her face.

"And your aunt, she is very angry at life. Don't take it personally. There's much healing to be done in the family because

this craziness needs to stop with you, Sari. You're the one w̶
the strength to begin it."

Sari looked exasperated with the request. As Heimy's energy
began to fade, he mentioned one last thing, "Oh, and ask your
mother about your brother."

"I don't have a brother," Sari said incredulously.

"Well, you do. Your mother had him a year and a half before
she had you. She put him up for adoption. You should talk to
her. It will help both of you. I'm very proud of you, Sari,"
Heimy said, before his energy receded completely.

A bit overwhelmed by the disclosure of the secret of her
brother, I stumbled through my words to Sari. "You should ver-
ify what he said for yourself. I'm just the messenger," I advised.

"Thank you. Yes, I'll find the right time to talk with her
about it."

We were speechless for a moment, gazing at one another,
hearts wide open, smiling, bathed in the transcendent charge
thick in the room. I inhaled deeply with reverence of what had
just occurred.

Several months passed before I received a call from Sari.
She called to recount a recent visit she'd had with her
mother.

"You're not going to believe this, Daniel. We visited a spa in
the hot springs. I began to tell my mother about you and
Heimy. You were right. My grandfather's name was Heimy, not
Joseph, my mom explained. I told her about the dog and the
other things Heimy said, and she seemed entertained by the
whole story, but didn't seem to take it too seriously. I was
relieved that she was able to hear it without thinking I was
crazy.

"It wasn't until later that night after dinner that I mentioned
the other part, the part I was afraid to ask. When I mentioned
a brother, my mother became stone silent, the kind of silence
that screams so loud it's paralyzing. Now, I thought, she really
must think I'm nuts, so I made a disclaimer: 'It doesn't necessarily mean literally. It could mean a symbolic brother, or a mis-
carriage or something like that.'

"My mother said, 'I don't want to talk about it.'

"It was silent all the way back to the room. Once inside, I
finally said that I was so sorry I had brought it up, but I knew

ething to it. Mother cried for quite some time,
le, she began to speak again.

n when I was seventeen and gave him up for
said. 'No one but my stepmother and step-aunt
And neither one of them is still alive. So no one
knows. Not my sister, not your father, no one!'

"We both sobbed as she told me the story," Sari said. "My mother began to speak again after catching her breath: 'It was like another life, one that I had buried, until my dog, my baby Jessie died, and it brought up all my loss.'

"Out of nowhere, my mother's pain seemed to ignite again. 'It's none of their damn business! I'm mad at those spirits for poking into my private affairs,' my mother protested.

"Now, it was my mother's turn to feel bad for burdening me. She has suffered through so much loss and pain, and I felt bad for bringing it up. But I know it helped," Sari said. "Her face looked as though a burden had been lifted."

In a subsequent session together, Sari's grandfather made his presence known again, and he told me a name and a location for her brother. When I relayed this to Sari, she responded, "I would love to meet him, and I hope he seeks us out. My mother said that if he found us, she wouldn't reject him, but she wouldn't go searching for him either. I feel I must do the same out of respect for her."

Sari told me that since the day her grandfather first visited her, she still feels his presence once in a while, almost as if some door has been opened. Since that time, Sari found her soul mate, and they started a family together. Sari and her husband, Jimmy, now have two beautiful children, a boy and a girl. And they did end up moving back to be close to Sari's family. Sari told me that it's not all that she had hoped it would be, being that close to the family, and that they're still working out many issues. But she's happy that her kids can grow up knowing their grandparents because family is family.

This episode blew me wide open. It caused my neck to lock up for two weeks. After I spoke with Sari, I realized I couldn't have been reading her mind because she had no knowledge of a brother. Suddenly, all my beliefs about life and death were up for re-evaluation. Over the years, Spirit has continued to nudge me along in spite of my resistance and doubt. Now that I'm comfortable with conveying the messages, the beauty of the healing can speak for itself.

Spanky

Telepathy is a phenomenon that occurs when we experience a break in the normal mind chatter and become available to hear communication beyond the five senses, as in the case of my client who brought her dog to see me.

The door opened, and he walked right up to me as if to say, "All right, let's do this." He looked like a cross between a Rottweiler and a pit bull. He stood mid-height, solid muscle and sparse short white and brown hair, and weighed about eighty pounds. Spanky had a rough beginning, his owner, Jakki, relayed to me. Apparently, he had been used as bait in dogfights when he was just a puppy. A gang member gave him to Jakki, telling her that this puppy was too sweet to be involved in that sort of thing.

It was love at first petting since then for the past eight years. Jakki was being treated herself for some blocked energy issues. She mentioned that her dog had problems after being kicked by a cow on a camping trip. The veterinarian reported that he would only get worse in time, and there was nothing more he could do.

Jakki brought him to me to see if I could help after I had mentioned that I had some experience with animals. I placed my hands on his neck and chest. After a moment, I felt a huge gush of energy being released from his chest. He immediately laid down and fell asleep. It felt as though he had released the weight of the world. Jakki later reported that his legs were doing better and asked if she could bring him in for another session.

I knelt down on the floor and once again placed my hands on Spanky, and I immediately heard him say telepathically, "She moved my bed, and I don't like it! Please tell her to put it back and stop moving things around the house. It's making me nervous. Tell her I'm a lot more sensitive than she thinks, and I need more of a consistent schedule."

I could hardly believe what I was hearing. I had been communicating with spirits for years, but I had never had an animal communicate so clearly with me. I slowly looked up at Jakki and asked her, "Did you move his bed?"

She looked at me incredulously and burst out laughing, covering her mouth.

"Oh, my God, did he tell you that?"

"Yes, and he wants you to stop moving things around and be more consistent with his schedule because you're making him nervous. He's very sensitive, you know."

Jakki told me that the night before, at bedtime, Spanky didn't want to get into his bed, and he kept staring at her as if he were trying to tell her something. She didn't know what was wrong. He finally went into his bed after releasing a prodigious sigh.

"That's what he was trying to tell me, and I just didn't get it," Jakki said.

A few weeks later, Jakki brought Spanky to see me once again. This time, something was wrong. He kept walking in circles. The veterinarian said he had encephalitis, a condition in which the brain swells and causes pressure and pain. The doctor prescribed steroids, which only helped minimally. He also suspected that Spanky had cancer and suggested that he might be at the end of the road. Jakki hoped that I could talk with him and find out what was going on, maybe give him some relief.

Spanky was very clear with me. He said that he had fulfilled why he had come—to assist Jakki.

"It's true," Jakki said. "I don't think I would have made it these past ten years if it wasn't for Spanky. He has been my savior."

The next few days were very difficult for Jakki as she made the decision to put Spanky to sleep. She came to see me a week later and asked if I had been in touch with him. I said no, but just then his spirit came to me. His big, happy face became very clear. He showed me that he was chasing his tail, and she confirmed that he used to do that when he was a puppy. Then he told me a story of when he had a sharp pain in his left front paw, and how she had carried him.

"Yes, he was digging in the ground and got a red ant between the pads of his left front paw. It was biting him, and he was jumping around."

He told this story to confirm to Jakki that his soul was still around. He then told me that he had been like a father to Jakki to help her with the difficult transition of losing her father.

With each new experience like this, it continues to expand our awareness beyond the normal routine and opens the door to allow us to enjoy the miracles that happen all the time right before our eyes.

Drink

A pirouette of light unfolds within this mystical glass from
     which you partake
Savor the sensation of this human taste
Be well pleased in your adventure for you have created it
     to fulfill your soul's greatest desire
The full realization of love!

—Daniel Ryan

Chapter 5

Spirit Orchestration

He is dead in this world who has no belief in another.

—Johann Wolfgang von Goethe

People often have their own specific ideas about the spiritual dimension. More often than not, spirits orchestrate phenomena that actually provide greater validation of this realm than people are prepared to recognize. There are vastly broader implications of connecting with the spiritual realm that are beyond the simple message you may be receiving. Once you have connected with the spiritual realm, it will open the door for greater experiences to occur. There is a higher power at work facilitating an actual expansion of consciousness for all who participate in it. This will ultimately open your eyes to the inter-connectedness of all beings.

Blue Blanket

One pristine autumn day, I was looking out my window while enjoying a phone conservation with my friend, Nikki. The rain had just cleared, and the sky was crisp and clean with billowing white cumulus clouds painted across the sky. Nikki had just received a phone call from her friend, Veronica, who had given her some sad news: Their mutual friend, Charlene, had died the previous day. Although Nikki hadn't seen Charlene for a few years, they had grown up together and knew one another's families well.

Charlene had become a quadriplegic three years prior as a result of being thrown from her car in a severe accident. Thirty-five years of age and confined to a wheelchair, she lived with her mother, who was a nurse. Charlene made her way out the door in her electric wheelchair and ended up in the pool, where she drowned. I was listening to the story and enjoying the beautiful view when a spirit's face appeared before me, which I thought might be Charlene. I asked Nikki if Charlene had had pretty blue eyes and wavy blonde hair.

"No, oh no, I'm not talking to her," she said.

Nikki knew that I was a medium, but had yet to have a personal experience with it.

"You don't have to talk with her if you don't want to," I casually replied.

So we changed the subject for a few minutes until Nikki eventually said, "Okay, I'll talk to her."

"Well, let's see what she has to say," I said.

As I centered my attention on the spirit, the connection became stronger, and Charlene began to speak to me telepathically. She spoke rapidly and was eager to speak with Nikki. I had to ask her to slow down so it would be easier for me to understand.

"Do you remember when we used to go to McCormick's after we played softball? Wasn't that so much fun?" she asked Nikki.

"Now I know I'm really talking to Charlene because there's no way you would know that," Nikki answered with anxious excitement.

"There are some things I would like to share with my family. Can you please write them down?" Charlene asked.

Nikki seemed hesitant at the prospect of sharing this message with the family. She had known them most of her life, but wasn't sure how they would respond to something like this. I had learned all too well through my own experiences that even a person in your own family can hold vastly different belief systems. We all come into this world with our unique expressions of the soul.

Charlene continued, "Now, first of all, tell Bill to quit being an ass and just marry her. And, Jasmine, I'm really looking forward to playing with your daughter. To Dad, I never told you enough, but you were always a really great dad. And Mom, when I was in the hospital in a coma, I heard what you were saying to Kathleen as you tucked the blue blanket over my shoulders."

Charlene's personal communication to the family meant little to Nikki because she hadn't been around the family for so long, but she wrote it down carefully anyway, as requested.

Then Nikki cautiously asked, "So, how are you doing, Charlene?"

"Oh, Nikki, I'm able to run and dance again. It's awesome."

Nikki then pleaded through her tears, "You want me to give this to your family, but how can I do it without looking like a freak?"

"Give it to Bill at my memorial. He'll know what to do," Charlene said.

Charlene's memorial was held at the local park that the families had frequented over the years. There were many memories of the good times juxtaposed with grief hanging in the air like smoke, choking people up. As a testament to her vast humanitarian interest, people of all ages and walks of life were in attendance. Pictures displayed her sparkle and sense of humor. Nikki later explained to me that there was a barbecue, but she couldn't remember what she ate because the emotional environment was so poignant.

Charlene had known that Bill would be the most receptive to her message from the spiritual dimension, and she turned out to be right. After the service and away from the others, Nikki approached Bill.

She explained, "I know this sounds weird, Bill, but I have a friend who's a medium, and when I was talking with him a few days ago, Charlene started to speak to him. I took some notes on what she wanted to tell the family. I have it here. She said I should give it to you."

"Absolutely," Bill said.

Bill had been interested in the idea of life after death. Although he was nervous, he was also excited and insisted that he read it immediately. Laughing out loud, his eyes sparkled as he read.

"That brat! She still got the last word. Of all the things she could have said, she's telling me to just marry my girlfriend? She's been saying that for years!"

He continued to laugh. "Thank you so much, Nikki. I'll share it with the family when the timing is right. I have felt Charlene around, you know, and I've been looking for a sign that she's okay. In fact, she did give us a sign last night. The whole family was at the beach to spread her ashes and do a special ceremony for Charlene. We asked her to give us a sign that she could hear us. We all gathered around the fire to say a prayer, and as we lifted our heads and opened our eyes, there was a shape of a big heart burning in the log. We all gasped at the same time. It was very clear. It burned independently of the rest of the fire, and then, after a few minutes, the heart once again became a part of the larger flames. It was unbelievable. We all lost it after that, crying, laughing and hugging."

Three days after the funeral, Kathleen, Charlene's sister, called Nikki. She sounded shaken and had so many questions. She wanted to know how and where she had gotten all the information that she had given to Bill. She was especially interested to know if I had known what she and her mom were talking about when Charlene was in a coma and they covered her shoulders with the blue blanket.

Lastly, she asked, "And how did you know about me covering her shoulders with the blue blanket?" Her stoic façade began to crumble as she explained through her tears, "Her shoulders were always getting cold, and no one knew about the blue blanket except my mom and I. And why was there a message for everyone except Rachel?"

"I don't know," Nikki said. "Please don't be upset with me. I thought it might be important for the family to receive this message. That's all I know. I was just taking notes as I was speaking to my friend."

A few days later, I received a call from Kathleen, Rachel, and their mother. Their pain and anxiousness poured through the phone as they spoke.

"Can you contact Charlene again? Could we all come in together?"

Stifled by the raw emotion I felt blasting through the phone, I hesitated and took a deep breath.

"Yes, you're welcome to come in for a session, but I can't promise that she will come through again. It's not only up to me."

Just as I finished saying that, I felt Charlene talking to me again. She said that she would talk to them if they came in, but she would also like to talk to her mom in private.

When I calmly explained this to them, I heard silence, the kind of silence you hear after a gasp. I knew they were still on the line, so I waited a couple of moments before asking, "Is that okay with you?"

Kathleen stammered, "We'll have to give you a call back after we talk about it."

That was the last I've heard from them. I could feel that there was a hidden message in there from Charlene intended for the family members only. Spirits often will not communicate a message in a way one expects, which usually provides an even greater validation for the intended person from the spiritual realm. I got the feeling that they heard the complete message that they needed during that phone call. I was curious to know what was said, but I could feel that that door was closed, and it wasn't about me, so I didn't inquire any further.

As for Nikki, she was concerned that she had upset the family, but was so relieved that Charlene talked about how she could dance again. She became very emotional as she recounted the last time she saw Charlene.

"It was horrible moment. She was in a wheelchair with a metal brace holding up her head and a plastic tube connected to her throat. But now I can hold the vision of her dancing with a windswept smile across her face."

I could hear Nikki sniffling on the other end.

"Are you okay?" I asked.

"You know, just the thought of her going through all the pain and limitation in her life really got me. She was a great athlete, and to see her limited to life in a wheelchair upset me to no end. If this could happen to her, it could happen to anyone. Holding the vision of her dancing and smiling again lifts such a burden from me. I am so thankful."

The memory that Nikki had of Charlene had imprisoned

that energy in her, but during the course of communication between them, the stagnant energy was released, and she could now think of Charlene in a different light. Just as our thoughts and feelings toward others affect them, so it is in the spiritual realm. Nikki's having a more positive vision of Charlene's spirit also benefits Charlene. Messengers are chosen for a reason. Nikki was chosen here, and she was being healed as well.

In the following scenario, Carrie's life shifted as she broke through her armor and allowed Spirit to facilitate a new direction for her life.

The Yogi

Carrie appeared to be a strong and intelligent woman. She had a voice to be reckoned with. She knew her job well and could handle just about any situation with confidence. This had served her well in Hollywood, working as a prominent movie producer. After working relentlessly for years, she arrived at the top of the ladder, only to discover that she was climbing the wrong wall. She was referred to me out to help her with this crisis. As I worked with her and, without her realizing it, she was starting to break down internally. I witnessed her stoic exterior break and saw signs of weakness unraveling before me. When she looked into my eyes, I looked back into hers, wet with surrender, her vision blurry.

Her body shook, and her voice cracked as she spoke. "Wow, it felt like a surge of love and tenderness just rippled through my body."

The release of tears and sweat dampened her blouse because of the catharsis she had experienced in the previous thirty minutes, supine on the table. The cold steel cell that had imprisoned her heart most of her life began to melt. Her identity dripped to the floor. Carrie sought me out to help her with the restriction she was feeling in her body that had gripped her over the past year and a half as her responsibilities as a movie producer weighed more and more heavily upon her. Carrie was being forced to struggle against a new identity that was yearning to be birthed within her.

I had worked with her several times prior to this day, witnessing a gradual unraveling of her intricately woven defense mechanisms in the process. They were appropriately placed as a child, but now were a hindrance to her. She told me that her "picker" was broken. She kept picking unhealthy relationships, and she wanted to change. As a child, she had been separated from her siblings and ushered from foster home to foster home. The state had taken her and her siblings away at an early age, due to the incompetence of her parents. Her mother was a drug addict, and her father was missing.

While I worked on her, I could feel and guide her through the thick, murky waters of the stagnant cellular memories that had kept her emotionally bound and isolated most of her life. I had learned to decipher what I was feeling from what others were feeling as a survival mechanism that served me well in my own childhood. Her body became still once again. The rhythm of our breath synchronized momentarily. A guiding, loving energy appeared above her. He was one of her guides. His black hair and olive skin framed his wise, shamanic presence. Heavy ritualistic symbols hung around his thick neck with an eagle feather peacefully at the center. His mysterious, luminous eyes changed color as he spoke of Carrie's shamanic potential. He told me she was destined to accept her path as a modern shaman to guide others on their journeys.

When I explained this to Carrie, she replied sarcastically, "That's what I was afraid of." We both chuckled.

During her sessions Carrie let go of multiple blinding layers of negative energy, which enabled her to catch a soul vision for her life path. I had communicated with other guides before, but this was not the norm. My particular ability had been connecting people with friends, family, and loved ones who had passed. Over the next few minutes, the room grew very still, with only our quiet, restful breath making any sound at all. Just then, another energy appeared to me. His spirit slowly came into focus.

His symmetrical bald head framed his large, vibrant, mystical blue eyes. He communicated easily with me. His energy was clear and peacefully evolved. Just as it is here in the physical realm, it is easier to communicate with certain spirits, depending on how evolved the soul is and if they have completely accepted where they are.

The spirit's name was Michael, and he was very loved and respected within the yogi community by those who had the honor and privilege of knowing him. Carrie, being in the mode of utter surrender, welcomed the communication. I told her that the spirit said his name was Michael, and I described him. Her face exploded with excitement and revelation.

"Oh, Dan, that's Anya's husband you're talking to. A terrible thing just happened last week. My friends Anya and Michael were involved in an auto accident with a motorcyclist, and after they pulled over to exchange information, the other man attacked Michael. The man shoved Michael so hard that he fell back and hit his head on the curb. Michael sustained a severe head injury and died in the hospital after being in a coma for a few days."

I have observed how spirits will arrange contact with specific individuals via the most direct connection. Since Carrie knew Anya and Michael, Michael used me as a medium to get a message to Anya. Michael had a very detailed message to convey to Anya. First, he wanted her to know that he was in a serene place and not to worry. In fact, he wanted her to know that how she thinks of him affects him. Consequently, he emphasized how important it is that she knows how well he is, and that she holds positive visions of him in her heart.

I continued to relay the message from Michael for Carrie to relay to Anya: "I want you to continue with the plans we made to adopt a baby girl from a Chinese orphanage. And please don't worry about my funeral so much. Just cremate my body and spread the ashes over our favorite lake."

Carrie released a quiet gasp when she heard this message.

"He means Lake Cachuma. We were all there together just a few months ago for a yoga retreat," Carrie explained.

As Michael's energy began to fade, he said, "I love you, Anya, and I'll talk to you soon."

Carrie's eyes met mine with sweet surrender. The smile in our eyes and mouths rose slowly and brightly. Carrie was excited to relay the message to Anya, saying she would call her as soon as she got home. Later that week, I received a call from Anya asking if I could contact Michael again for her.

I responded, "Well, I can't guarantee who will show up, but we can certainly put in a request."

When Anya arrived, she greeted me with a tentative warm smile and apprehensive crystal-blue eyes. Anya was a tall, slender woman, with short yellow hair and distinct German features. She had migrated to America to complete her residency as a surgeon. Traditionally trained in allopathic medicine, I sensed some reservation to my holistic approach. But, apparently, her acute grief and desperation for answers won out over any preconceived notions.

Over a course of several sessions, I shared in a series of unilateral conversations; I relayed what Michael wished to communicate to Anya. Often, the spirit will answer the questions and concerns the person has before they actually verbalize them. During our sessions, Anya would laugh, cry, look peaceful, be angry, and smile, but rarely spoke to me about it.

During this time, the messages I conveyed from Michael were in great detail about meditation, breathing, healing energy, different dimensions, continuing the process of adoption, love, surrender and the peace of God. This was a new experience for me because people usually tell me the significance of what was said after the session, but Anya did not. In one of our final sessions together, I asked her about her experience with our time together, and she said, "It has been the most profound and healing experience that has ever happened to me."

The last time I saw Anya, her face was calm, and her chest and shoulders were open.

"Thank you for your gift," she said, as her being seemed to move in peaceful acceptance. She continued to release the grief and accept her new life, just as Carrie accepted her intuitive guidance to change her life path as well. In one of our sessions together, Carrie said, "I can't do it anymore. I have to leave the business. I no longer buy into Hollywood's or society's idea of what authentic wealth is."

Carrie stopped producing movies and decided to follow her intuition to become an acupuncturist. This process took about a year and a half before she began graduate school, which took three years to complete. It was difficult for her to make the transition from being well established in her career and making a large income to becoming a poor student. But she came to a point where she felt like she no longer had a choice. Carrie realized that the evolution of her soul was not about obtaining, but releasing, allowing, and becoming more herself. This is a common struggle along the spiritual path and actually a sign of spiritual maturity. She had overcome her fear of being vulnerable enough to trust her intuition and follow it for the first time in her life.

As a healer, she could no longer hide behind an identity. True healers know how crucial it is to get out of the way of their identities, to create an open vessel for infinite wisdom to enter. Carrie said she felt at peace knowing she was following her soul's intention and well on her path toward self-realization.

Later, Carrie came back to see me, not for a session this time, but to see clients in the same room in which she had the healing experience, I smiled and responded, "That would be fine, but you must remember that it's not the specific room that facilitated your healing, but your consciousness and intention to do so. That will always be with you wherever you are."

By completely accepting where she was in the moment, the change was able to begin. The evolution continues. She is still allowing her identity to unfold. Carrie no longer has the illusion that she will reach a point where she will be done. That kind of linear thought process is incongruent with a natural expansion of consciousness, which is spherical.

Chapter 6

Validation

If a man does not find peace within himself,
it is useless to seek it elsewhere.

—*French Proverb*

The age-old dilemma of facing one's mortality is addressed in the next story. Mark, a client of mine, had previously endured an arduous break-up with a woman he had hoped to start a family with shortly after they married. At forty-four years old, he was questioning the meaning of it all. But the mystery of the soul's existence was settled for Mark when he put his questions insistently out to the universe. It was no accident that a significant role model appeared at such a time to give him faith again. Mark received validation far beyond what he expected because he remained open. His experience touches on the transformation a person can experience when they have confirmation and resolution from a deceased loved one.

The Holy Grail

One day, I was hiking up in the mountains when I felt my barometer shift, a familiar feeling I get when a spirit is attempting to get my attention. It was as if the weather was changing, and a refreshing breeze blew right through me. Mentally, I became very still to receive the message. A woman in her sixties with short, curly brown hair and blue eyes came into focus. Her lips revealed her stern disposition and the discomfort of a heavy body. She told me she was here to see Mark, a client scheduled for the next day. This wasn't that unusual as spirits sometimes get excited about making contact, and they start talking to me up to a week or two before I even meet the person they want to contact.

I have to admit that when Mark came to see me the next day, I was a bit hesitant to mention it to him. He looked like a "show-me-the-facts" kind of guy. Standing 6'1" and just about as thick with solid muscle, this hockey-player-turned-TV-host was a bit intimidating. I balanced his energy and he looked quite relaxed with a content smile on his face. After finishing our session, I almost said good-bye without mentioning the spirit that I sensed in the room, but something stopped me and turned me to face him once again with a quizzical look.

"Do you ever feel any spirits around you?" I asked.

"Not really, but I would like to. Why? Do you see any spirits around me?" he replied.

"Well, actually, I do. There is a woman here with curly brown hair and glasses."

"Younger or older?" he asked.

"Older, and she is showing me a cookie," I said.

He exploded in laughter. "That's my aunt who passed a year and a half ago. Her nickname was Cookie. She was my godmother."

"She's showing me a huge heart in her chest, which symbolizes how much she loves you."

Like a Salvador Dali painting, spirits will often use symbols as one way to communicate.

"I love her the same way. I was closer to her than anyone in the family. I've wanted to re-connect with her since she passed. The two of us enjoyed a deep psychic connection. In fact, we used to play telepathic games together, guessing what the other was thinking. Quite often, we would be right."

Just then, Mark's head fell forward, and his right hand reached up. His fingers squeezed his eyebrows together as he began to recall the night Cookie passed.

"The worst thing was that I was traveling and felt that I needed to call her. An alarm was going off in my head to call, but I didn't, and she died later that day. I didn't follow my intuition. My brother Dan called me at 1:30 a.m. to give me the message that she had died. I always felt terrible about that." He paused, fighting back the tears, wrestling with his reddening face. After a few moments and several deep breaths, he regained his composure before continuing.

"I know that she went quickly and didn't suffer much, but I should have been there for her. She was my best friend from the day I was born. We had such a deep soul connection. I wasn't sure about life after death, even though I wanted to believe it existed. I felt like a part of me was missing when she passed. Cookie promised me she would contact me after she passed to let me know that she was okay, but I didn't hear from her until now."

As Mark was talking, I could see Cookie listening with contently with a loving smile.

"She's telling me that she's your mother's sister."

Mark became exhilarated. "Yes, yes. I've been trying to contact her since she passed, just after my forty-third birthday. In fact, that's the real reason I came to you originally a year ago. My girlfriend told me you had contacted her mother who had passed, but I never mentioned it to you. I thought I would just see what you had to say, but you never brought it up when I came to you before."

"Well, spirits come through when everyone is ready," I said.

"Ask her what her nickname was for me," Mark said. "If she can tell you that, it will remove any doubt in my mind that it is her."

"Doesn't hurt to try," I said, so I asked Cookie telepathically if she could tell me the nickname.

"I've asked her three times, and she's not responding. In fact, the more I ask, the more irritated she gets. She keeps saying this name, but it doesn't feel like the name you want to hear. It doesn't feel like your nickname."

"What is it?" Mark asked.

"She's insisting that I tell you the name Rocco."

"That's amazing! That removes any doubt in my mind," he replied.

"Is that the nickname she had for you?"

"No, it's her maiden name and her father's last name. In fact, believe it or not, her father even lived on a street named Rocco!" he said, laughing with elation. "That's not my last name, and there's no way you could have known that. Come to think of it, if you had told me the nickname, I would have wondered if you were reading my mind because I was thinking it so hard for her to hear while you were asking her. And her getting impatient with you, well, that was totally her personality, too. She was a sweetheart, but was known to get frustrated and impatient rather quickly with people."

I explained to Mark that spirits give validation, but they give it on their own terms and for good reason, as she had done in this case.

"Maybe it was because she knew that you would have doubted it, thinking that I was just reading your mind."

"How can I continue this connection with Cookie?" Mark asked.

Cookie hesitated for a moment and then replied, "Do you remember when you were thirteen years old, and you came to me to talk about your troubles?"

Mark replied in surprise, "Yes, I do."

Cookie continued, "Well, at that moment, our connection deepened, and our souls formed a special bond that will never be broken. When you remember this feeling, it will bring you home, and you won't need anyone else to help you because you have the capacity to do it on your own."

Mark's eyes widened all of a sudden. "Oh, wow, I feel as if wind is blowing right through my body, and it's tingling all over. Do you feel that?" he asked.

I laughed. "Yes, I feel that often. It's the energy of the spirit moving through you. Oh, and one more thing, she's showing me a black hat. Cookie started to tell me how much she loves you, but then she stopped as she thought it unnecessary."

"Yes," he said, "I feel the same way. We got to share all the great things in life and not the crappy things. I'm so relieved that she is still with us and doing so well. I wanted to believe in life after death, but I wasn't sure. I needed proof. Thank you so much. Wow, I feel so much lighter now."

He paused for a moment.

"Black hat?" he pondered.

"If it doesn't ring a bell now, remember it, and it may make sense later," I said.

"You know, this is like finding the Holy Grail."

I asked him to explain.

"Well, ultimately, what is people's greatest fear? The fear of mortality, right? Well, if you can communicate with the spirits and provide validation of life beyond the limitations of our physical bodies, what more could you ask for? That's it, right? It's like finding the Holy Grail."

"Yes, you're right," I said.

I really enjoyed watching Mark's reaction to re-connecting with his aunt. Mark had become disillusioned after losing her. But making contact lit a fire in his eyes that had long been extinguished. It gave him validation of life beyond this physical realm. For me, I had an epiphany, and it actually motivated me to continue writing down these stories. I knew that if Mark had been moved so deeply, this would be inspirational to others as well.

We said our good-byes. As Mark left, I noticed that he had an extra spring in his step.

Mark called me a few months later, eager to talk about the "black hat." He had been looking everywhere for a sign of a black hat, but didn't see it. Finally, he was going back home to get together with the family and thought maybe someone there would be wearing one, but it was nowhere to be seen. After the meal, while the whole family was sitting around talking, his mother brought out presents for the brothers. They all opened them at the same time. Inside the boxes were matching black baseball hats with a "D" inscribed on them, signifying the first letter of their last name.

Mark thought, "Oh, great. All I need is a black hat with a big 'D' on it."

Just then, his girlfriend came into the room and gasped. She looked at Mark and pointed to the picture on the wall of Cookie with a big smile on her face.

Chapter 7

Openness

The last enemy that will be destroyed is death.

—1 Corinthians 15:26

The stories in this chapter convey how we need to be open to the message, even if it is not from whom we expect. Spirits are often trying to help, often in mysterious ways. Once we release our expectations, the highest and clearest communication comes forth very naturally. We need to help them help us!

Murder Mystery Solved

Gabrielle had the kind of heart that's skittish: in search of a safe place to land, but only when conditions are just right. When she came into see me for an appointment, she had just endured yet another break-up with her boyfriend of five years.

"I think it's really over this time," she said after years of this emotional roller-coaster ride.

Because I had the pleasure of knowing both her and her boyfriend, she asked for my opinion. I knew they shared a deep love for one another, but they lacked the tools to manage the relationship in the long run. Gabrielle had had enough of this pattern. After seeing it repeat itself, she was over it. I encouraged her to continue to open her heart and trust the intuitive direction it would take. Over time, I helped her achieve this direction by balancing her physically and energetically. This also helped balance her emotional and spiritual state of being.

This day was a better day, unlike the previous few weeks when mere eye contact brought forth tears, as she would say, "Don't look at me like that. I don't want to talk about it."

She had improved. She was healing. Acceptance tiptoed in, and her anxiety had diminished. This day, we had a visitor. I was concentrating on shifting the energy around her heart chakra, when this spirit eased in like a warm breeze, gentle and reassuring. Her hair flowed back from her forehead in a black, silver, and white wave. She told me she was Gabrielle's maternal grandmother. Gabrielle confirmed this with a slow nod, not offering further information. Her grandmother said she was there to watch over and protect her. Gabrielle was interested, but not overly excited. I asked if she wanted to ask her anything.

"Yes, ask her about Ginny," Gabrielle responded.

As soon as she asked the question, the spirit of another woman came forth, and the grandmother's energy receded. I described the woman to Gabrielle. "She has short brown hair, brown eyes, and a positive energetic personality," I said.

"Yep, that's Aunt Ginny all right."

"She has something she wants to straighten out with you. She says that the family has long suspected her boyfriend of murdering her," I said.

Gabrielle lost her composure with this revelation. Her eyes reddened, and tears welled up immediately. Her voice struggled to explain.

"Yes, that's true. The whole family still suspects he did it, even though they caught another man, who is now in jail."

"I know he was an abusive, angry man in the past, but I want you to know that he was innocent. They arrested the right man," Ginny said.

"That's incredible. Everyone thought her boyfriend did it because of his history of being abusive."

The energy hung in the room like a dark cloud, gradually opening to the sun.

"It's okay to breathe," I said, and we laughed. "Would you like to ask your grandmother anything else?"

"Yes, how about Uncle Geoff? Is he around?"

I felt a heavy, hazy feeling creep into the room, but I didn't see anyone.

I waited. I began to get the feeling that Geoff had been strung out on drugs and alcohol as he gradually appeared to me. His dark, wavy, tousled hair failed to hide his weary demeanor. Pasty white skin followed the furrows of a man who had lost the fight, but I saw a spark of redemption in his eyes as he spoke. He talked of the dear woman before me who stayed by his side the last six months of his life. His face softened as his love for Gabrielle came through.

"I want you to know how much I love you, Gabrielle, and I want to thank you for helping me in those final stages."

Gabrielle's face suddenly opened like a new day. She was completely present, vulnerable, and open.

"I helped him die," she whispered through joyful tears. "It was the most enlightened but difficult thing I have ever done."

Geoff continued, "You taught me so much about love just by the way you stayed with me. It was incredibly healing."

"No, thank *you*, Geoff. You've helped me let myself love," Gabrielle said. "Geoff, I want to know if we did you right by the way we handled the funeral."

I spoke. "Geoff's showing me ashes blowing in the wind. He says he was cremated."

"Yes," said Gabrielle, with a huge smile, "I've spread his ashes all over the world."

"Well, Geoff is showing me a thumbs-up, so I guess you did the right thing."

Gabrielle's face relaxed, and her eyes smiled. It appeared that Geoff would continue his unraveling and revealing from the spiritual realm, while Gabrielle would trust her heart more each day here in the human experience.

Spirits have mentioned to me in the past that transformation is an easier process while one is in a physical incarnation as opposed to being in the spiritual realm. Apparently the lessons are more tangible with the physical density. I have found many people to be perplexed by this notion because it seems to be a common belief that once you shed the mortal coil, your soul is completely free of any further challenges. It's hard to know the depth of healing as souls reconnect, but to witness the reconnection is magic that has the power to transform the physical realm.

Double Murder

John was referred to me by his sister, Vicky. Vicky came to see me for the sole purpose of contacting her father, who had passed two years prior. Vicky initially didn't mention why she came in, but she did say that she felt uncomfortable with "this type of thing." The puzzle began to come together as she lay on the table.

On that day, the spirit of her father appeared before me. He had a large, shiny forehead. His large brown eyes demanded my attention. He said he had messages for Vicky, her brother, and her mother. Vicky said that she still had tremendous pain over her father's death. She had only come to me because her cousin had convinced her that I could help her contact her father and solve the mystery of his death. It had been two years since that morning when her father disappeared after a family dispute. The next time they would see him was in the morgue. Vicky wanted answers: What happened? Was he murdered? Who did it?

When her father appeared to me, he explained that he had been robbed and died resisting the thieves. He told me his heart collapsed during the altercation, and his memory of the rest of the details became vague after he had been struck in the head.

After we finished, Vicky lay quiet and nervous, absorbing the new information. Being presented with information that was incongruent with her current belief systems proved to be quite challenging for her. Attempting to comprehend what had transpired, she politely left my studio.

I didn't hear from her until four months later, when she called to tell me how much I had helped her accept her father's death and also helped her mother to accept his passing. She didn't tell her brother, John, about the session until months later. Interested in his sister's experience, John felt compelled to see me right away.

When John came in, I assumed that he wanted to speak to his father as well, but that's not the way it turned out. John had thick black hair, deep olive skin, and kind and sensitive hazel eyes. He was a handsome man in his mid-thirties, standing about 5'10" with a humble and sincere demeanor. Almost immediately after we began our session, a man about fifty-five years old appeared to me. He had a mostly bald head with some hair combed over the top. He was round, overweight, and short. When I described him, John said that he wasn't sure who this spirit was. Because of his sister's experience, I think we were both expecting his father to come through again, but this certainly wasn't his father.

I continued, "He's showing me that he was shot in the left shoulder. The bullet pierced his heart, killing him instantly."

With a quick breath, John's eyes opened wide. "That must be Arthur!" he exclaimed. John's eyes filled with grief that spilled down his face. After attempting to collect his composure, John explained, "He used to work for me."

I saw another spirit of a much younger and leaner man with thick chestnut hair and deep walnut eyes. "That's Frank," John recalled. He had been with Arthur when they were killed. John's voice fell off in despair. "It was over a car. I own a car lot, and some gang members shot them just to steal a car. It was just a car."

Arthur had a wife and son to whom he was anxious to convey a message. He wanted them to know that his spirit had continued on, and he was watching over them always. Frank had a son of whom he was very proud. He told his son that he was the head of the household now and knew he would take great care of the family. Yet another spirit came forth as Arthur and Frank's spirits receded. This was turning into a party.

He was striking, with thick black hair with a silver streak through it like an exclamation point accenting his presence. John again didn't recognize him. I asked the spirit who he was, and he said that he was Frank's father. He said that his daughter, Frank's sister, was still very angry and wanted revenge. He wanted John to give her a message. John agreed. He urged her to let it go and move on, that he was in a good place, and all this anger was eating away at her. Arthur was not in such a good place. He was having trouble accepting his transition, but assured me he would be fine in time.

About thirty minutes passed, and I thought that would be it. Then the spirit of John's father came forward to speak to John. The first thing he said was that they were in a fight right before he died, and it wasn't John's fault. He told John that he loved him and had completely forgiven him long ago. It was now time for John to be free and be his own man, free of regret.

The session with John lasted for about forty-five minutes, which seemed like ten. I immediately wrote down this story after he left so as not to forget the details and feelings. In the past, I have learned that I will often forget the details of these communications, and sometimes I will forget that the whole event occurred if I don't record it or write it down. This happens because I am in an altered state, and I am not using my logical mind to process the information.

Chapter 8

Prophecy

The body without a soul is no longer at the sacrifice.
At the day of death it comes to rebirth.
The divine spirit will make the soul rejoice
seeing the eternity of the world.

—*Nostradamus*

The experiences in this chapter are examples of how prophetic messages emerge and prove to be accurate over time. "Bubba," the story of the unfathomable heartbreak of losing a child, reveals the redemptive joy that occurs when a child's soul reincarnates with his parents. "The Window Beyond" demonstrates the mystery and accuracy of a spirit's prediction of his son's lung cancer and how it came to pass.

Bubba

The blue and white porcelain kitchen tile appeared especially crisp that sunny Southern California morning. The spring spilled in through the windows with all the promise of rebirth and rejuvenation in the air. I was completely immersed in the moment. The phone rang; everything changed. Andrea and Richard, our dear friends and the godparents to our daughter, were about to give birth to their first baby. They fondly referred to their son-to-be as Bubba.

Richard and Andrea had met on a photo shoot. Richard, a successful, high-profile fashion photographer, and Andrea, a stunning, all-American blonde-haired, blue-eyed top model and actress, were a sight to be seen.

Due to previous medical complications, it was necessary for them to implement in-vitro fertilization to conceive. Finally, after several attempts and spending a small fortune, Andrea became pregnant. Andrea requested our presence at the birth. Her labor had begun a few hours earlier. Excitement filled our home as my wife and I waited for the opportunity to assist her in natural childbirth. On the table, turkey bacon and hot steel-cut Irish oatmeal, cradled in white china, were waiting to be eaten.

I felt a mixture of suspense and elation as I reached for the ringing phone. It was Richard. He was frantic, unable to complete a sentence. "Andrea's bleeding. The baby stopped moving." They were on the way to the hospital. My heart fell into my stomach. I was no longer hungry, but sick.

The baby didn't make it. I felt my body turn inside out in a primal attempt to rid itself of the wrenching sadness. My tears fell and broke the smooth surface of the milk in the bowl of oatmeal.

Ominous clouds, threatening rain, filled the sky the night before the funeral. Thunder woke me, or so I thought. As I rubbed my eyes, I sensed a very strong persistent presence in the room. It was Bubba's spirit. He insisted that I write down a poem to read at the funeral. I squinted to see the clock. It was 2:15 a.m.

"Can't it wait until six?" I replied.

"No, please write it down now. It's very important." I transcribed his poem in my notebook:

*I remember when God exhaled, and I became a sparkle in
   your eyes*
I remember how my spirit never dies
*I remember when your gentle hearts reached out to catch
   me as I became of this earth*

I remember divine love and joy as the miracle grew inside
* you*
I remember that night when your body and soul shuddered
* with disbelief beyond human understanding*
I remember when your hearts poured out from your eyes,
* forming a vibrant river of love with all eternity*
I remember the deepening of the richness of your souls as
* the gifts continue to unfold*
I remember how my spirit transcended my body, and unto
* God I was released*
I remember that God granted us all perfect peace
I am, I am the oneness

In the sea of sorrow that filled the tiny chapel, I tried to breathe deeply. The time came for me to speak. I briefly explained that the poem was a message from Bubba. His strength guided my voice as the words lifted the veil of my finite mind. The black attire, black coffee, and chocolate cake were offered to quiet the pain in the room that was yearning to be released. This ritual was just the beginning of the healing process to follow. A long journey of healing lay ahead.

During this time, I recalled one particular session with Andrea. It had been during her pregnancy with Bubba, and her grandmother's spirit came for a visit. Andrea's grandmother had said, "You will have so much fun playing with your little girl."

But this didn't make sense later when the doctor proclaimed, "It looks like a boy to me." It would be years to come before it would make sense.

A few years of healing passed before Andrea and Richard were ready to try again. They were successful, and this time Andrea's grandmother was right: It was a happy, healthy baby girl, just as she had predicted.

With my hand above Andrea's belly, I felt the vibrant energy of the baby during the pregnancy. I was surprised by the message the baby conveyed. She requested to be named Gabriella, and Andrea and Richard loved the name as well, so it came to pass.

Meanwhile, Bubba's spirit had come through to me many times since his passing, to console Andrea and Richard with their loss, and also to reaffirm his existence. Even after Gabriella's birth, Richard and Andrea continued to long for little Bubba. One day, Bubba revealed in a session, "I'll be back, but it's not going to look like you expect."

Andrea's face lit up as she said, "I'm pregnant again. I'm so happy . . . and scared."

Early on, a blood test revealed that they would be having a boy this time. Andrea was exhilarated with the news. But the sky fell when she learned that she was going to have another girl and that the earlier test had been wrong. Andrea and Richard had held the hope that Bubba would reincarnate and come back to them, as Bubba had said.

Nonetheless, they were grateful to have a healthy baby, regardless of its gender. Little Angelina arrived into welcoming, loving arms, with her happy, healthy, vibrant spirit. At three months of age, while holding her, I could feel that Bubba's soul was indeed in little Angelina. I mentioned this to Andrea. Her eyes reddened. As her mouth searched for air, she attempted to respond. "You know, we have a picture of Bubba we took when he was born, and Angelina looks exactly like him," she said.

"This must have been what Bubba meant when he said that it wouldn't look like you expect," I said.

This incredible revelation came to us on Father's Day, and it also happened to be the anniversary of Bubba's passing. We knew that it wasn't just a coincidence. So often it appears that things are orchestrated from the spiritual dimension contrary to what one would expect. This oftentimes offers an even greater validation. Andrea and Richard's lives continue to unfold with their beautiful, loving, energetic girls. They attempt to take one day, one moment at a time, in gratitude.

The Window Beyond

Kasha had been my client for seven years. Originally, she sought me out to help her heal from what she described as a "less than idealistic upbringing." As we got to know one another, we became friends and shared an interest in energy patterns of the body, as well as the phenomena of the spirit world. Kasha worked as a massage therapist and liked to practice tuning into people energetically. I helped her heal much of the stagnant energetic patterns that had been dormant within her most of her life.

Physical manifestation of pain always lies somewhere in the broad spectrum of being predominantly physical or emotional. In Kasha's case, I found her to be leaning toward the extreme emotional end of the scale. With a narcissistic, alcoholic mother and a father who abandoned her at the age of three, Kasha was practically left to fend for herself, navigating her way through childhood without much of a support system.

Under her mask of feeble confidence lay a foundation built on insecurity, unreliability and indifference, which were often not so well hid by her cantankerous demeanor. Encased within her transparent harsh exterior lay a wounded little girl crying out for help. Rather than align to the vibration created by her current restrictive energy patterns, I held her to the greatness of her un-manifested potential, while unconditionally accepting her current state. At times, she would project anger toward me, lashing out harshly. Other times, she would unravel into a puddle of grief, which looked impossible for her to escape.

Fortunately, I held my ground, not taking any of it personally. This built a deep trust between us. While she was in my studio one day, a very interesting thing happened. She was face down on the table with my hands on her back as I assessed her energetic condition. As I tuned in with my eyes closed, I could feel a cool breeze pass through my body. Suddenly, a face appeared before me. My whole being became very still as I was showered with a tingling energy that fell right through me. A tear swelled in my right eye, threatening to be freed. At that point, I was completely open and receptive. Before me stood a small man, with large benevolent eyes, reminiscent of Gandhi. His stature was loving and sincere.

As he communicated with me, all five senses merged as one. There was no separation. I could actually feel, hear, taste, smell and see what he was saying all together.

He said he was Kasha's great-grandfather, who had died of a heart attack twenty-three years before. He wanted to convey a message about her grandfather, his son, to Kasha.

He told me a date and continued his message: "Your grandfather will become ill with cancer in his lungs. Resist any treatment until it's too late, and there will be nothing you can do about it."

I have always felt uncomfortable conveying prophetic messages from the other side, but I did, regardless, since I had a trusting relationship with Kasha. But, of course, this was notwithstanding my disclaimer, "I'm just the messenger and please have him evaluated by his doctor."

He continued, "He will be stubborn, and it won't help if you try to force him to get help."

I asked him why he was telling her this. He replied, "I want to help soften the blow to Kasha and, more importantly, to confirm that my soul is alive and well in the spirit world."

Along with the message from her grandfather, I witnessed a luminescent purple energy being sent by him into Kasha. It appeared to be transforming her on a cellular level, making her feel lighter to me. The energy in the room was so transcendent it was palpable. Our eyes met, and we broke out in laughter, dissipating the intensity of it all. This helped me to remember not to take myself so seriously.

I followed by saying, "Don't look at me. I'm just repeating what I'm hearing. Check it out for yourself."

Kasha hardly knew her great-grandfather, but she wrote down the message anyway. It was a year and a half before the date he gave. When we met again, Kasha explained that she felt much lighter and had become much more sensitive since that day. She explained that now when she worked doing hands-on healing, she was seeing and feeling incredible things she had no way of knowing. With the emancipation of the stagnant cellular memories within her, it opened and strengthened her intuition. She was getting out of the way of herself and acting as a clearer channel for healing energy to come through. This was the happiest and most passionate I had ever seen her. Life seemed to be getting easier. When the call came from Kasha in March 2003, the date he had predicted, we hadn't talked in a few months, and I had since forgotten about the communication with her grandfather.

"You're really good, you know. You won't believe what happened."

She began to convey the details of the past couple of months. Her grandfather was in the hospital with Stage Four lung cancer. He was admitted after waiting six weeks to get his shortness of breath checked out. He later passed within two weeks. A chill ran through my body and the hair follicles stood at attention on my arms after hearing news of this confirmation from the spirit world. I am always grateful when I witness the miracles that are constantly unfolding.

At my core, I feel it is our destiny to open our perception, to see what actually is. This is naturally done with meditation and pure intention to the universe for it to happen. This great cosmic unified field then conspires in our favor to manifest our soul's intention. This incident inspired Kasha to deepen her own spiritual practice and enhance her natural intuition.

The Circle of Life

The midnight breaks, the dawn falls upon our shoulders
The first light washes the soul
My mind beckons, I do not comply
Forever lost in the magic, I am content in my undoing
Falling, the undeniable sensation of the wind rushing
*   through my hair*
The dance of divinity I feel before my eyes
No pretense, no pressure, no possibility of control
The freedom unfolds the surprise as coming upon a daisy
A smile, a thousand smiles pour through
Sweet deliverance from our self-perpetuated confinement
The decision is to live, not through a mundane existence
But an ecstatic dance of divine alchemy
So it is the circle of life is always complete in its expression

—Daniel Ryan

Chapter 9

Forgiveness

Holding on to anger is like grasping a hot coal
with the intent of throwing it at someone else;
you are the one who gets burned.

—*Buddha*

It may be difficult to fathom forgiveness in certain situations, but having the intention to forgive and release the energy is the first step toward freedom—one's own freedom. This step opens the door for Spirit to broaden our perspective and purpose, which may have previously seemed inconceivable. This is the beginning of allowing Spirit to help us forgive others and ourselves.

When Mickey came in to see me, he didn't expect to be made a believer through the message of forgiveness from his late wife of fifty years. And when Angie came for energy balancing, the last thing she expected was that the spirit of the person who had killed her husband in a reckless head-on collision would be asking for her forgiveness. Then there was Gina, who simply wanted to be unstuck, not realizing that the lack of forgiveness for her late father was a major component of her inability to move forward in life. In the final story of this chapter, my client recounts her experience of forgiving her father and the synchronicity of the timing with her sister.

I Drink Spirits

In all of his ninety-three years, he had not believed in any existence beyond the physical realm. He loved the sea and had spent the past thirty-five years sailing and power boating as much as possible. Standing about 5'5" with fiery green eyes and an old brown leather bomber jacket for skin, Mickey wouldn't be fooled. He spoke as though he had wrestled the world victoriously, absent of any regret. Life had rounded his shoulders and sharpened his mind.

Mickey propelled himself forward in a slow, rigid gait like a steam locomotive, building momentum. Unfortunately, he became almost completely immobile as a result of an unsuccessful surgery on his lower back the prior year. The surgery was intended to relieve pain and restriction.

The doctors told him that his back had just worn out, and there wasn't any more he could do. In fact, he wouldn't be able to walk any longer without a walker. But Mickey wasn't going to accept that for an answer. So he continued to exercise by swimming and walking in the pool, in spite of his restriction and pain.

I instantly liked him. His sandpaper demeanor smoothed out all the peripheral noise and allowed heart-to-heart honesty. Mickey was all pistol. I learned during the course of a few sessions that he had always been an athlete and enjoyed a keen interest in women.

"I've always been very active with the ladies," he proudly boasted. He had become a multi-millionaire due to his astute business sense and the good fortune of inheriting the family business. After World War II, his father started making lampshades out of his garage. He turned this business into the most successful manufacturer of lampshades in the U.S. in just fifteen years' time.

"I heard you talk to spirits," he said with a skeptical grin he wore as an old winter coat.

"Do you have someone you want to talk to?" I replied.

"Ah, I don't believe in that crap," he said with a single wave of his hand, dismissing any and all things beyond the tangible realm of the five senses.

"You don't believe that spirits exist?" I inquired, smiling.

He shouted back, "I drink spirits!"

Our laughter shattered the brief silence.

Not to be detoured so easily, I prodded, "Seriously, what do you think happens to us when we die?"

An impish smile grew across his face. He was five years old again as he sang out of key, making his point explicitly clear. "The worms crawl in; the worms crawl out."

"What am I going to do with you?" I pleaded through my laughter.

"How about you just make me feel better, and I'll be happy."

His current wife, Charlotte, twenty-nine years his junior, had sent Mickey in to see me as a last resort before he had yet another surgery. Charlotte originally came to me to see if I could help her with some energetic restrictions she had suffered for the past seven years. During one of the sessions, the spirit of her mother appeared to me. She had passed two years prior and left many unanswered questions for Charlotte, which, in her words, had "jaded her perception of love." Charlotte experienced healing closure and a new perspective after we were able to communicate with her mother, who expressed remorse for not being a better mother. She also reassured Charlotte that she had learned quite a bit going through her transition. Most important was the fact that her soul continued on after her body ceased to exist. Charlotte had had a difficult childhood, with her father being killed at a young age in the service and her mother being an emotionally unavailable alcoholic. She was left to fend for herself as an only child.

Charlotte met Mickey at a yacht club and enjoyed being taken care of, as well as taking care of Mickey. Charlotte had been a nurse for many years and "knew what she was doing," said Mickey. She enjoyed his confidence and fortitude. Mickey's persona preceded him, making him larger than life— at least larger than 5'5" anyway. We began our session together after he was finished speaking his mind.

"Well, let's have a look," I said, as he lay down on the table. As I navigated through the stern skepticisms that wove a web of constrictions throughout his energy field, I felt a presence in the room. Her hair was a windswept golden yellow that draped just above her shoulders. Her eyes told a story of surrender from a life of being married to this man firmly invested in his ideology.

"There is a woman named Helga here who says she was married to you for a long time."

"Oh, yeah," he snapped back sarcastically. "What does she have to say?"

"She says she forgives you," I replied.

"Ah, I don't believe in that crap," he said in his old seaman voice that had been whipped by the sea breeze enough in his life not to be convinced that easily.

That was the very abrupt end of that conversation until his next visit, when he stood tall and faced me, firmly anchored in his disbelief, and blurted out, "What specifically does she forgive me for anyway?"

Unaffected by his demeanor, I attempted to align my focus to communicate with Helga. I relayed the question to her telepathically and, fortunately, she was again present and responded instantly.

I confronted Mickey with the question, "Are you sure you want to know?"

"Yeah, give it to me. Let's see what she has to say."

"Helga says that she forgives you for the redhead, the brunettes, and the blonde."

Mickey's quick-witted mouth fell open. All color drained from his face as the mask disappeared from his eyes. His whole being surrendered, and his eyes reddened. It appeared as if any disbelief escaped him instantly. He stood motionless, dumbfounded, and amazed. His eyes swelled with the love overflowing from his heart.

"She is the only one. The only woman I ever loved. We were married for sixty-one years, you know."

"Wow, that's incredible. She wants you to know that she felt no pain at the end, and felt completely resolved and at peace those last few hours when the doctors disconnected all the machines," I said quietly.

"I hated seeing her go through that chemotherapy. It almost killed me," Mickey confided.

Helga continued, "All is well, and I'm free now, Mickey. You were always a good man. I don't want to make you feel bad. It's time to let go for now, but I'll see you again."

His tear-stained cheek closed the final chapter of their tumultuous bond of love. Mickey's chest stood at attention, releasing a sigh of relief.

"Thank you, Doc. Thanks for everything. Hey, what do you know, I feel a lot better! "

"You're welcome, I think. You should thank Helga as well."

I knew that Helga was instrumental in the healing of Mickey's heart with the power of the love that she had sent during the process. As Mickey was leaving that day, two beautiful women walked by the hallway and continued to his right. Mickey paused, and then took a step, following them.

"The elevator is to the left, Mickey," I reminded him. Mickey stopped and slowly looked back over his shoulder with an impish grin while pointing to the right and said, "I know, but I want to go that way."

Angie

This story begins on a mountaintop. I found myself immersed in the crisp beauty of the yellow daisies dancing in the heavenly breeze, carrying the aroma of lavender and jasmine, which was eager to greet me. It was one of those days when all things feel possible. The water tumbled and rolled down the spring creek, creating a constant rhythm with the symphony of blue jays, sparrows, crickets, and frogs.

I heard a voice, as if someone were whispering. A tingling sensation climbed up my neck to the top of my head. A whoosh of energy went right through me. I recognized this sensation as that of a spirit wanting to make its presence known. Just within my peripheral vision, an energetic silhouette of a spirit slowly turned his face toward me. I was taken off-guard, but remained receptive.

It's a myth that spirits only appear in old, haunted houses after midnight with ominous clouds brewing and doors creaking. A spirit can deliver a message right smack in the middle of a beautiful day. As the connection increased, the spirit's features came into view. He was a large man, square like a linebacker, standing about 6'1", with thick, dark brown hair and matching bushy eyebrows. Pale white skin framed his deep green eyes. His tenacity commanded my full attention.

"You will be seeing my wife in a few days, and I wanted to introduce myself in advance to see if I could help in any way," he said.

His intensity slightly repelled me. I acknowledged him and said, "It will be fine to contact me later, but right now I am not available. Will you please wait until she comes into my studio to continue?"

At this point, I still didn't know who this spirit was referring to when he spoke of "his wife." I would later learn that he was a computer whiz, who had done well in the tech world. He had purchased a home with his wife, Angie, with the intention of starting a family together.

A few days after her husband came to me, Angie arrived for her session. Her olive skin accentuated sea foam green eyes, framed by thick, curly, energetic auburn locks. She was the kind of woman who knew her beauty, but was utterly unconcerned about it. During our first meeting together, her raw vulnerability was a step ahead of her. Angie explained that her husband had died in a car accident a few years before. Her pain was palpable, with a well of tears always threatening to break free. Angie had finally found her soul mate only to have him ripped away after one year of marriage. Her girlfriend, a client of mine, convinced her to contact me, saying that she was certain that I could help her to open her heart again. After only a few minutes into our session, she began to lean forward in her seat. Her hair fell over her hands, which were cradling her face. There was only silence, except for some sniffling from her.

Slowly looking up, her grief-filled eyes spilled tears onto her cheeks.

"I don't know why I'm crying," she sobbed.

I attempted to put her at ease. "Not to worry, you're processing, and it's good," I said as gently as possible.

I had her lie on the table supine as I began to untangle the delicate web of defense mechanisms she bore emotionally and energetically. It felt dark, convoluted, and constricted as if I were trying to swim through a murky swamp underwater with my eyes open. My hands repelled slightly.

Fortunately, Angie was face down on the table and unable to witness this. I explained the process: "We're not trying to fix anything, but simply using the power of our presence to illuminate the truth. That which is not true about you will fall away in the process."

Angie nodded quietly in agreement. She reassured me in the beginning to please share with her any messages I may have, that she was ready to heal. She took a few deep breaths while I removed negative energetic patterns from her body. Suddenly, a spirit's face appeared before me. His eyes were wide open, and his head shook. I was confused at this point because he didn't resemble the spirit I expected, that of her husband, the one I had seen up in the mountains. His yellow hair, blue eyes, and youthful appearance resembled a surfer. He spoke rapidly, eyes erratically darting side to side.

"I was the driver of the car that killed your husband," he blurted out. I described him to Angie and relayed what he said.

The air in the room became dense. "Oh, God, that is him. His name was Mark."

Angie's quivering voice attempted to explain. "My husband was killed in a head-on car collision five years ago. A reckless driver on crystal meth and alcohol was chasing his girlfriend, lost control, and slammed into my husband's car, killing both of them instantly."

Mark began speaking again, pleading. "Please, forgive me. It was such a stupid thing that I did. It tore apart your family and mine."

A moment of silence passed before he continued, exhausted from the intensity of his emotional plea.

"He's telling me the numbers 26 and 27," I said.

She replied softly, "I was 26 and Mark, the driver of the other car that killed my husband, was 27 at the time of the crash. I can't do this." Angie froze, her body tensed.

"We can stop at any time if you are uncomfortable," I reassured her.

After a few deep breaths, her shoulders dropped and she said, "I think I'm okay now. We can continue."

"Please find it in your heart to forgive me," Mark pleaded once again, pausing between phrases. "Also, It's important that you know that I was driving my father's car at the time of the accident."

When Mark said that, Angie abruptly burst out crying once again. Her hands whitened around the arm of the chair, as if it was all she could do to hang on. Now panting, I hoped she wouldn't hyperventilate. I considered stopping the session at this point, more concerned about Angie's welfare than Mark's emotional plea. It appeared to me that this was new territory in her healing process. After a few moments of silence, her breath slowed and she lifted her head to speak.

Angie explained, "The insurance policy was a disputed fact in court that influenced the outcome of the civil lawsuit that ensued after the accident. If he were, in fact, driving his father's car at the time of the accident, then the burden of financial liability would be upon his father and his father's insurance company, which had much better coverage."

This specific information was extremely valuable to Angie. "I just don't know if I can forgive him," Angie confided in me in a quiet, little girl voice, as if Mark couldn't hear.

Mark's spirit began to fade, and another spirit came forth. This one I recognized as her husband, who had approached me before at the mountains. I described him to her, and she shook her head rapidly, saying "no."

Now I was confused again because he had said that he was her husband, and I thought she would want to speak to him. She began breathing deeply again and eventually confirmed that it was her husband, Roger, but that she just got overwhelmed again and needed a moment.

"Okay, I think I'm all right now."

I continued, "He's showing me where he was fatally injured. His head and neck are swollen and contorted."

"Yes, that's right," she sighed.

"How did this happen?" Roger snapped back, with furrows forming in his forehead as his face angrily screwed tighter. He paused for a few moments and then slowed down as he addressed Angie once again. "We need to heal this together, Angie."

When I relayed this to her, she nodded her head "yes" through the tissues.

"I don't think that either of us can heal until we let it go," Roger said.

"I don't know if I can let you go," she said.

The fact that Roger was disembodied was irrelevant; he had healing to do. This confirmed further that the soul continues to evolve even after a physical death. I invited Roger to join us in the future when Angie came in, and they both thought that was a wonderful idea to continue this healing process together. Over the next few weeks, Angie continued to heal the open emotional wound the accident had left her. She started working with a non-profit organization that helped abandoned children find new families.

On subsequent visits, she continued to find her peace, although it was a long, difficult journey for her, one that forever changed her view of mortality. Angie became much more interested in finding the gift that was always right in front of her, especially the depth of joy she received when she spent time with children.

Hoping to be a mother herself one day proved to be a positive impetus to the continued expansion of her ability to love. Eventually, the children she worked with became her new family. Opening her heart to these children allowed her to begin to forgive the man who took her husband's life.

Gina

Gina stood as I entered the room, her eyes cast downward. Her words came from somewhere between hope and desperation.

"I came to see you because I knew you could help me," she said. Her innate joy could no longer be subdued by the despair that had haunted her most of her twenty-two years. It was time to be released. The open curves of her dark walnut hair fell to her mid-back. Standing 5'9", her slim Swedish-Italian beauty was incompatible with the emotional weight she so laboriously bore from her father's abandonment of her.

The energetic constriction in her upper back was sudden as a train wreck, and destined to be as fatal if not addressed.

Gina said that she felt that the power of her intention to heal had illuminated the shadows and provided her with divine guidance. She had begun to fight back against her eating disorder and alcoholic tendencies on her journey of healing. She was combining weekly psychotherapy with a twelve-step support group.

Although well on her way to recovery, she needed additional assistance to purge the stagnant energetic density in her body. I felt moved by Spirit to give her extra special attention. When this occurs, I feel as though an agreement deep within me is being honored, and it's very gratifying. Gina's frank honesty with me created a clean slate to begin our process together.

A couple of days before my first session with Gina, a young spirit had made his presence known. He wanted to contact her through me. I asked him to please visit again when she came to see me, which he did. During that visit, he stood slightly hunched, with dark hair, dark eyes, and a mild look of disdain, holding a cigarette in his hand. His presence was a bit ominous to behold and uncomfortable to experience.

Often, spirits will show me how people remembered them physically to further the validation for the sitter. He had similar features to Gina, suggesting a possible genetic link that would later be revealed. When I described this young spirit to her, she said that she didn't know anyone who had passed and didn't know who I was describing. In the past when this would happen, I would sometimes question the validity of what I was hearing and seeing. But through my years of experience, I've come to understand that the message is always perfect, even though the communication is not. Consequently, when something doesn't make sense at the moment, I don't worry about it. I know it will be revealed in time.

A few moments later, another male figure came forth. He had a large, round face, and thinning dark hair on top of his head, framing his distant brown eyes.

"That's my father you're describing," she said. "I never knew him. He left when I was only two and a half, but that's just what he looked like in the pictures I have of him. I don't know why he would come back now, since he never did when he was alive. My mom said he was a rat. I don't know what to say to him."

"Your father actually has some things to say to you. He says he has a brother, your uncle."

"Yes, that's right. He's still alive."

"He's telling me that the young spirit trying to communicate with us is Ricky, your uncle's son, who died in a car accident."

"Oh, God, yes, he was on a motorcycle and was hit by a car. My cousin Ricky was always getting into trouble. He was a real 'bad boy type' and always hung out with people who were up to no good."

"Apparently, he is drawn to you because you have had similar challenges, and he thinks you can help each other heal. He says that you understand one another."

I didn't know what issues he was referring to, but I assumed they were very similar to Gina's patterns, in addition to the ones he mentioned.

"Okay, sure, that would be cool, but does this always happen? Is there something else I should know? I mean, I don't know what to think about this. Can it happen this quickly?"

"It's always different," I replied.

Gina accepted the spirit communication without much difficulty, eager to resolve the conflicts within her and earnestly willing to try almost anything to relieve her physical and emotional pain. This allowed her not to overanalyze this phenomenon, which ultimately removed her as an obstacle to her own healing and allowed the transformation to quicken.

"Now your father wants to talk to you about your mother. Is that okay with you?"

"Well, okay, I guess so."

"He says that he's not the 'terrible guy' your mother portrayed him to be."

"I always thought he was a bad guy from the things my mother said."

"Your mother had a lot of issues that she never talked about, and I think you should know to help you understand why it turned out the way it did. You see, your mother had been sexually abused when she was younger, which greatly affected our relationship. She pushed me away, but I wasn't the warmest person either, and maybe that's why we attracted each other to begin with. But I'm sorry that it caused you so much hardship. I'm so sorry, Gina. I know it was wrong. I love you. Please forgive me for leaving if you can."

Gina's head fell forward, and she fell silent. A few minutes passed before she lifted her head. She spoke softly, and a tear rolled down her cheek.

"How can I do that? I mean, he just up and left and never even tried to contact me. What kind of father is that? He wasn't there to see me ride a bike for the first time at Christmas time, or when I had pneumonia and had to stay in the hospital, or when I graduated from high school. I needed him. I needed his guidance, support, and, most of all, his love. How could he say that he loves me when he just disappeared? How can I forgive him?"

"Forgiveness is your path to unraveling the family legacy wrapped around your natural joy. This is not only about your father. Forgiveness is for you just as much as it is for your father. In fact, most forgiveness is self-forgiveness. It can be the key that will open and free your heart again," I said. "When you set the intention to forgive, even if you cannot fathom it, the universe will conspire in your favor to assist you in your endeavor."

Gina gradually smiled. "I don't know if I can, but I'm willing to give it a try. You know, I feel so much lighter. Wow, when can I come back? I want to continue this work with you. It's awesome."

Her father and cousin's energies began to fade. Gina understood that this epiphany was merely the beginning. With greater clarity and self-acceptance, Gina knew she had an arduous task ahead of her, keeping her addictive tendencies at bay. Gina left that day with a renewed enthusiasm to embrace life and the fortitude to move forward to trust and fulfill her intuitive direction.

A Sister's Pain

[The following story is told in the words of a client of mine who wrote this experience down for me.—D.R.]

One morning, I woke up with an octopus wrapped around my heart. My life was upside-down. I was feeling less than courageous. I rummaged through my purse and found Daniel Ryan's name, which I had gotten from an enthusiastic man and his wife soaking in a natural hot pool at Two Bunch Palms.

Hours later, I was lying facedown on Daniel's table, my face on shiny paper wedged in the face cradle. In his inimitable gentleness, Daniel said, "Your father is here. He's asking for your forgiveness." My father had taken his life ten years earlier

My father told me that my sister wasn't doing well. He had

a lot to be sorry for and needed her forgiveness. And he wasn't happy that I had become estranged from my mom over the holidays, which was true. He asked me to stay close to her. He then repeated over and over the name of a man that my husband was flying to see at that very moment.

My mind was racing around the room. I asked myself, "What does this have to do with energy blockages in my body?" But, in a moment, I understood that this was how I had felt a long time ago as a little girl—young, scared, and overwhelmed. Daniel asked if I was ready to release my father and the impressions that were lingering in my body. I was more than ready. I left Daniel that day feeling more like myself. I felt spacious, openhearted, hopeful, and trusting that everything was going to work out. I was also pain-free. My body felt connected again.

The next morning, I called my sister, who hadn't spoken to me in nine months. Surprisingly, she picked up the phone. I explained that I had seen Daniel for the first time for energy balancing, and that our dad had shown up and was concerned that she wasn't well. I told her that he was sorry and needed her forgiveness. She interrupted me and asked, "What time was this?" I told her it was around 4:00 p.m. She had been in her car at that same time, and felt our father near her. She said out loud in the car, "I can never forgive you."

I gave her Daniel's number and encouraged her to see him. I hope she does so she can feel the peace and well being I am experiencing as a result of working with Daniel and whoever else shows up.

Forgiven

Through a very large crack
A tear emerges
Then another
And another
From the blackness emerges the pain
Anger, fear, self-righteousness and blame
The light illuminates the shadow
The crack opens further
It is a much larger heart
Ageless and timeless
Eyelids fall
The corners of my mouth reach up to greet them
The sweet release of remembrance
All is forgiven

—Daniel Ryan

Chapter 10

Danger

*The greater danger for most of us lies
not in setting our aim too high and falling short,
but in setting our aim too low and achieving our mark.*

—*Michelangelo*

We are always guided along by the wisdom of the ages through intuition and divine guidance from the spiritual realm. At times, it takes extreme measures to get our attention as in the next story, "Saved from a Fire." The multigenerational healing that transpired as a result was dramatic. And when Eric returned to connect with his friends in "Cheetos and Sprite," it sent a powerful healing message throughout the community regarding the safety of our youth.

Saved from a Fire

By the time they smelled the smoke, the flames had already escaped the electrical panel and begun to devour the foundation in the basement of this historic 1920s Craftsman home. Within three minutes, the fire trucks arrived to rescue this landmark home with minimal damage.

Later, Diane had a local handyman fix the electrical breaker box and install new wiring. Diane had grown up in this house and moved back in after her mother, Rose, passed two years before. Rose had lived in the house for more than fifty years. She was the much-loved and revered matriarch of the O'Brian family, and was missed dearly.

This fire was news to Kelly, Rose's granddaughter and Diane's daughter, who had come to see me for a healing session. Kelly was feeling a bit out of sorts and wanted me to balance her energy. I had seen her several times before. When I do energy balancing, I close my eyes and allow my intuition to guide my hands to the areas that are in need of balancing. As I have my hands on or above an area, images and feelings come to me empathically. Most of the time, it isn't necessary to talk to the person about the balancing because the combination of the power of my attention and the individual's clears the problem. As the person's mind quiets while focusing on breathing, the space created helps release the aberrant energy patterns.

If these stagnant, outdated belief systems are not illuminated and dissipated, they create energy blockages and subconsciously influence the choices we make. They permit confusion to enter our lives and distort our ability to understand how these situations arise.

During this particular session with Kelly, I felt an intense, vivid presence in the room. An old woman in a wheelchair appeared. She wore a smile from another lifetime that accentuated the depth of her pale Caribbean-blue eyes, like a warm ocean wrapping around me, holding me peacefully.

Suddenly, her demeanor began to change. As she became intensely somber, she began to speak to me.

"I am Kelly's grandmother, Rose, and I have a message for her."

I gently repeated this to Kelly, who was instantly elated that Rose had come for a visit. Being very empathic and intuitive herself, Kelly had previous experience of feeling spirits and welcomed the communication.

I conveyed what Rose said. "Hello, dear. I need to talk to you about something that greatly concerns me."

"Hello, Rose. What is it?" Kelly replied anxiously.

Kelly's fingers began to circle one another as her eyebrows came together and her smile faded.

"There was a small fire under the kitchen in my house six months ago, and I'm worried that it didn't get fixed properly. Can you please tell your mom to get a licensed electrician out there to check it out? I'm afraid it's a fire hazard the way it is. I should have had it fixed twenty years ago. Will you please tell your mother to have it fixed right away?"

"Oh, that sounds scary. I'll make sure and follow up on that soon," Kelly said.

"Thank you, dear. What a relief."

After a moment of digesting what she had heard, Kelly asked, "How are you, Rose?"

"Oh, sweetie, I can dance again," she said with a timeless, loving smile. "I hated that wheelchair. It's so wonderful to be free to move about again! I didn't mean to scare you about the house; I just want to make sure that it gets taken care of. Tell your mom that I'm here with your father. Can you believe it? We're helping each other out now." Kelly later informed me that they weren't on good terms when Rose passed.

I witnessed Rose's loving kindness pour into Kelly from the spiritual realm. A wave of indigo-colored transcendental energy filled her. Her shoulders dropped with surrender and acceptance. It was beautiful to see Kelly's grandmother's loving energy embrace her, as if it were washing away all her frustrations. Kelly's face appeared as though she had just eased herself into a warm bath and had relaxed to the core. Kelly had had her share of challenging relationships and emotional struggles over the past few years, and to see her now so peacefully relaxed was a blessing.

"I love you, Kelly. You are awesome, and don't forget it!" said Rose. And just as gracefully as she came in, her energy began to fade.

"I love you, too, Rose. I'm so happy you're doing so well."

As I slowly opened my eyes, I still had one foot in the other dimension and felt completely at peace with a transcendent tingling flooding my body, a feeling that always feels fresh. Kelly gave me a hug, and her face told me she was feeling the same way. Before she left, she promised to get back to me after discussing the session with her mother, Diane.

Two weeks later, Kelly confirmed that there actually had been a small fire under the kitchen, and Diane hadn't mentioned it to her three daughters because she didn't want to worry them. She also didn't take the message from Rose seriously enough to hire another electrical contractor to fix the wiring properly.

Later, in another session with Kelly, Rose came through again to reiterate the importance of fixing the electrical panel.

Before leaving, Rose added, "And, oh, by the way, please tell your mom to get rid of that old blue wedding dress. I don't need it anymore!"

When Kelly gave her mother the most recent message from Rose, Diane sat up and took notice. It was a sobering revelation to her.

Kelly's mother had been cleaning out the house the week before and had come across the light blue wedding dress. She had hesitated to give it away because it had been Rose's. Diane had said a tearful prayer to her mom, asking, "Mom, what should I do? Should I let this dress go or hold onto it?" Rose responded to Diane's quandary about the blue wedding dress even though Kelly hadn't known anything about it. This made Diane a believer, and she had the electrical panel fixed properly. This validation of the existence of Rose's spirit prompted Kelly's mother to come in for a session as well.

Fortunately, Diane had a wonderful sense of closure with her mother when she came through again during her session. I could feel that much more than the fire issue had been resolved as Rose showered her with transcendental violet cosmic energy. As with most families, there were unresolved emotional issues that had an opportunity to be reconciled. Diane was relieved, and it gave her great peace to know that her mother was doing well. Her gratitude for this opportunity was humbling and gratifying as it once again validated the unique orchestration and persistence of the spiritual realm. Time and time again, I have witnessed that spirits want to come back to help us, as if they are cheering for us from the other side.

Cheetos and Sprite

It was a fresh spring day, and the air was full of inspiration. Loren and Dillon were both seniors at the local high school. When they arrived for their session their demeanors felt ominous, in stark contrast to their typical upbeat attitudes and playfulness.

"What's going on?" I asked.

Loren bent forward, covering her face and whimpering. Dillon's red eyes met mine and were filled with grief.

"My best friend died in a car accident last night," Dillon said.

I let the room breathe for a few minutes. I knew that this was not a situation that needed to be fixed at that moment, but processed over time. I had Dillon lay on the table and began to address his energy. I looked up at Loren, and next to her I saw the spirit of a young man with blue eyes, spiked blond hair and braces. I stopped working on Dillon and began talking to them both about what I was seeing.

"Did your friend have braces, spiked blond hair and blue eyes?" I asked. Loren's jaw dropped. Dillon slowly lifted his head off the table, looking at me incredulously.

"Yes, but how did you know?"

"I see him here in the room. He's standing next to Loren."

A hush came over the room, as if all the air suddenly escaped.

"He's showing me a Sprite and a bag of Cheetos. He says that was his favorite snack."

Loren immediately burst out sobbing. Dillon's hands grabbed his hair, his arms covering his face. As Dillon looked up, tears rolled down his cheeks.

"Eric was my best friend. He really is here, isn't he? I knew I felt him around, but I thought I must be imagining it."

"Yes, he absolutely is here, and he appears upbeat and happy. He doesn't want you to worry because he says he's doing just fine."

Loren continued sniffling intermittently, making brief moments of eye contact while her body attempted to find its way out of various awkward positions.

"He's saying that he's not sure how he got here. It all happened so fast. He was seeing how fast they could hang the turn, and the next thing he knew, he felt this terrible crushing sensation in his chest and left arm."

"He was in a car accident, and his car broadsided a tree. They were speeding," Dillon said.

"He's saying his chest got really warm, and he couldn't breathe."

"Yes, I know his chest was crushed in the impact," Dillon said.

"He's saying that the pain suddenly stopped, and he became very light. And he wants you to give his parents a message. 'Please tell them that I'm sorry.'"

After a couple of very long moments, Eric continued, as if he was trying to lighten things up.

"Hey, Dillon, the cool thing is that I can still hang out with you."

In the depth of their disbelief, I witnessed Eric reaching out to Dillon and Loren, sending them healing energy. The beautiful translucent violet-indigo energy wrapped around them, changing into a bright green as it began to free their grief. They both looked more relaxed and amazed that Eric had contacted them, but we all knew that it would be a long journey through their healing.

I found out later that Eric had gotten into an argument with his father right before he got into the accident that rendered him dead. He was a passenger in the car, and the boy who was driving lived, although he was in a coma for three months. It was an all-too-familiar story. Every year, high school students playing around and driving recklessly lose control of their vehicle and end up paralyzed or dead. This time, they had a chance to re-connect, and have some closure and healing.

Six months after the accident, Dillon told me that it changed his life. The sobering realization of what happened with his best friend made him re-evaluate his life's purpose and how he spent his time here in this precious incarnation. His intention was to live a life full of meaning and make a difference.

Chapter 11

Abuse

Darkness cannot drive out darkness; only light can do that.
Hate cannot drive out hate; only love can do that.

—*Martin Luther King, Jr.*

The actions born of unconsciousness often seem unfathomable. In this next story, Keefer finally has an opportunity to break the chain of dysfunction from his horrid past and allow healing to navigate his family to new horizons.

Burned

Keefer looked as tough as nails. Standing 5'11" and weighing a solid 200 pounds, Keefer had a thick hazel and silver moustache and eyebrows, and arms that looked as though they could throw some steel around. He had been resistant to getting help for his energetic and emotional challenges of the past ten years, but now was determined to take better care of himself.

"I've always been so busy taking care of everyone else. I never had time for me," Keefer explained.

He was an old fifty-two, weathered by his history of abuse and the intense manual labor of his construction trade.

"There was a wild fifteen years in there before I had my son, which I'm sure didn't help my body. Any way you can help, I'm open. I heard that what you do is different."

Beneath his deep bass voice and burly appearance, an extreme sensitivity was palpable. His tough appearance was only as thick as an eggshell and was beginning to crack, barely containing its fragile world.

As I listened carefully, I could feel the energy of his mother around him. Oftentimes, I see an image of the spirit's face first, but this time, I could only feel her. Her energy was tentative and remorseful. When her face did appear to me, it looked as though it had melted downward slightly like a used candle from the weight of the shame it held. She told me she had passed away about five years before and also mentioned the name "Elaine."

"Your mother passed away about five years ago," I said, more as a statement and confirmation than a question. He tilted his head to the side and squinted his eyes in disbelief. He said, "Yes, how did you know that?"

"I feel your mother's spirit around you. Do you ever feel her around you?"

"No. Yes. I mean, I don't know. I think maybe, but I'm not sure if it's just my imagination. Why would she . . . what does she . . . what?"

"We don't need to continue if you're not comfortable with this, but it feels like she has something she wants to tell you if that's okay."

"No, please, yes, continue. I want to hear what she has to say. I'm just surprised and confused about why she would want to contact me."

"She's saying that Elaine is here also. Does that mean anything to you?"

"Yes, that's my grandmother. She saved me from my mom when I was still in diapers. How would you know that name? I didn't tell you."

"Your mother just told me. And she just dropped her head in shame. She says that she doesn't begin to know how to tell you she's sorry. Your mother and grandmother are together, and they want to send you healing energy to help you. Is that alright with you?"

Keefer nodded his head as he leaned over with his hands covering his face. Unexpectedly, he wept. He was five years old again. As he spoke, I witnessed his mother and grandmother infuse him with a luminescent deep violet transcendental love and healing, a beauty that was beyond this world. It opened him up to speak and release the pain that he had harbored since childhood. His face softened and his shoulders dropped as he spoke of his experience.

"The state took me away from her. She was so abusive. . . . She burned my hands on the stove. . . . She would make me eat until I threw up while standing over me, threatening with a switch. . . . It was awful. . . . She was bi-polar. I understood better as I got older, but it was just hell. I basically grew up in a foster home. My parents divorced, and my dad left when I was very young."

I patiently witnessed Keefer shake as he attempted to find his way out of this vulnerability that had caught him by surprise and he was so obviously unaccustomed to.

I told him, "She said the name 'Elaine' so you could be sure that you knew your grandmother was with you as well. She knows that your grandmother was your saving grace. Your mother also wants you to help your sister to be strong and help you to not let her push you away."

"This is hard to believe. Did Mike tell you anything about me?"

"No, he didn't tell me anything about you, or even that he referred you."

Mike was his friend who had referred him to me.

"It's true, my sister is a mess, and she's so good at pushing me away that I've let her," he said.

I tried to explain. "I know it may seem strange, especially if this isn't something you're familiar with, but it's real. I've learned over the years that to help a person heal, it needs to be done holistically, from inside out. And it's okay if it doesn't make sense right now. But you can trust that a higher purpose and transformation are taking place. Can you trust that?"

"Yes, I guess so. I mean, this is hard to believe."

Keefer's mother and grandmother reached out to facilitate a healing between the three generations. Unless rectified, dysfunction has a tendency to pour down through the generations, continuing to perpetuate the pain. With healing and forgiveness, it stopped here. Keefer's son, eight years old at the time, had a chance to grow up in a much more balanced environment where love and security would allow him to develop a solid sense of self-esteem.

I believe I can best serve people when I get out of the way of the process and allow the healing to transpire. This is done most effectively by using my intuition and completely trusting what comes through. This is when I ask for the higher purpose of the person, and I follow it. There is no room for self-serving validation. It only impedes the process, regardless of how altruistic the intention. I sensed that this was the beginning for Keefer, and he now had a lightness that wasn't apparent before. A seed of new possibilities had been planted and was bound to grow and unfold from his new perspective.

Frozen

On many occasions, I've had the opportunity to help clients with a history of sexual abuse. Unfortunately, it has been estimated that one in four women have been subjected to sexual abuse. Amber's psychiatrist referred her to me. After a history of years of chipping away at her issue together in therapy, they both agreed energetic healing could further the process.

Amber was a beautiful young woman with chestnut hair, rich brown eyes and a smile that relaxed you with warmth. She exuded sexuality, which I would learn later was a large part of her identity. Women who have been hurt in such a manner need a safe environment to emote and build trust. This is vital in the healing process and is also a way to create a foundation for healthy relationships and self-esteem in the future.

"Dr. Morris said that there were other ways you could help me heal."

She didn't feel like she was in pain, nor did she feel like she was confused. Actually, it didn't feel like she was there at all. I heard her words. I understood what she was describing, but it was void of emotion, robotic even. As we continued our session, I realized that this is what she was feeling: frozen. It felt uncomfortable, disconnected and compartmentalized, as my hands sifted through the many energetic layers before me. I was feeling what she felt all the time.

I know you must be in there somewhere, I thought. I allowed Amber's energy to shift at its own pace until my hands ran into a cold, steel barricade of energy. It was a fort securely locked down, guarding her heart. It felt like this had occurred when she was thirteen years old. I asked her what happened at that age.

"That's when my brother died," she said. It fell out of her mouth and hit the floor like a stone. Heavy. I took a deep breath and exhaled.

Amber explained, "When I turned thirteen, I was sent to boarding school. It was an art school. My parents didn't know what to do with me when my brother, Mark, died. I guess they were trying to process their own grief as well. It was crazy at the boarding school; all the kids at school were doing drugs and having sex. It was a very liberal art school where the students were not monitored very closely."

I felt her body temperature increase as she released emotion. My hands were still a few inches above her body when the face of a boy's spirit appeared before me. He felt like her brother. He looked a lot like Amber: brown eyes, thick mahogany hair and bangs that extended from the part on the side of his head. He looked like a troubled child, with his head tilted slightly to the right. Easing my way into telling her about his presence, I asked her if she ever felt her brother around.

"No, I have always wanted to, but I don't."

From our previous conversations and my intuition, I sensed she was open to this communication, so I continued.

"I feel his spirit here. Would you like to talk to him?" I asked.

"Whoa, just before you asked me that, I actually did feel him around for the first time since he passed," she said.

Suddenly, an energetic shift happened as if the realization had just caught up with her. Amber choked and gasped for air, while making a feeble attempt to compose herself. The emotional environment changed rapidly, and her face became wet with grief. I asked if I should continue. She said yes.

"I asked him what his name was. It sounds like a name that starts with an 'A.' Wait, he's saying 'Angie.' Who's Angie?" I asked.

"That's me. My family called me that growing up. I haven't heard that in a long time."

Her tears appeared to wash away the old pain like water flowing across a watercolor painting. Her brother continued, "I know what Dad did to you. I'm so sorry that happened."

A long, quiet pause separated the revelations like the Grand Canyon, and then he spoke again. "He did weird stuff to me, too," her brother confessed.

"Mark's telling me that you have a deep soul connection and could help each other heal," I said.

"Yes, we always understood each other that way. I would like that."

Amber's eyes closed halfway, and her head fell back. Her shoulders dropped, releasing a long, deep sigh. As she threw her head back, I could feel her re-connect with her brother. When their energy came together, it changed from a red-orange to a deep violet color. The vibration quickened and became more translucent and light. While this occurred, it seemed as though their physical bodies became secondary while their spiritual bodies stood out.

Amber resigned to the revelation of the past by saying, "I always suspected that, but I could never confirm it. I don't remember much about my childhood, but I have all the symptoms of being molested: the sex dreams, obsessed about sex, my body image, etcetera, you know."

I actually didn't know, but I was learning, as I remained silent and allowed her to emote. A few moments passed. The room was breathing, energy swirling. I watched, but I didn't interrupt. When the time was right, I continued.

"I asked your brother how he died, but he didn't say."

"My brother started a fire in the garage, but then couldn't get out. He died of smoke inhalation. He started his first fire when he was only six years old. Then he was arrested when he was nine for burning down part of my school. He was always in trouble."

She spoke in a slow, somber tone. The energy in the room became more and more dense and uncomfortable until, suddenly, the room exploded with energy. When the stagnant energy patterns are released and the energy begins to flow again, it's always magical. After a few moments, the energy of her brother began to recede. Enough had been said for today, and Amber needed time to process it. She slowly rose, her inhalation lifting her.

Looking at me, she said, "It's no coincidence this happened today, you know. I'm catching a flight in one hour. I'm going to see my father. It's been a long time, and it's time."

Amber forced a weary half-smile. "My breath is lighter. That's different. It's always felt heavy to me," she said.

Because I was concerned about what had just transpired, I asked for her cell phone number to check in with her later that day. When I called, she spoke softly. She told me that she didn't expect her father to admit what he did, but it has certainly put things into perspective. I was concerned about my responsibility in conveying this message to her. She reassured me she had been working through this for years with her psychiatrist with much success, and this had merely been another confirmation.

On a subsequent visit, Amber expressed her frustration, particularly with her inability to connect on a deeper level with the people in her life. This was something she had always longed for.

"I don't trust anyone," she said.

"You trust me a little. That's a start," I said. "Let's try something."

I had her close her eyes and follow her breath down into her body and notice the physical sensations. Then I felt her attention go back up into her head.

"Whoops, you went back into your head. Nothing gets healed in the head," I explained. Amber smiled with surrender, and her face softened. I had her close her eyes and follow her breath down into her body again and just notice the physical sensations such as the rhythm of the expansion and contraction of her lungs.

After a moment of this, while I was standing a few feet in front of her and we were facing one another, I felt her vulnerability coming up. Tears rolled down her cheeks, and she shook slightly. She was not comfortable being vulnerable. She thought she needed to be strong to attack the fear and pain that she had harbored.

"Do you have that vulnerable feeling?" I asked. She nodded her head slowly up and down. "Accessing your vulnerability can empower you as a woman and help you keep your heart open. When your heart is open in the present moment, you have full access to your intuition. From this place, you can make the right decisions that will guide you in life. You become the flow of the universe. Thanks for trusting me, even if it's just a little."

Her face was a mess with wet mascara—a beautiful, joyful, smiling mess.

"Thanks for being trustworthy. You know, even though I have only known you a brief period, I feel like I know you better than some people that I have known for years," she said.

"I see you, you know," I said.

Her smile opened with the joy of being seen, arguably one of the most important things one can do in the healing process. To see and be seen is vital to validate a person's process on the healing journey. And so our journey continued. With the challenging opportunity of illuminating the dark corridors of her past, we had some work to do. Amber said that she was willing to accept the hard work ahead of her.

"This isn't easy digging through all this stuff, you know," she said.

"You're right. I've learned myself that the spiritual path is not for the weak," I said.

I've found it to be an interesting observation that one's pain is directly proportional to the resistance to feel the pain. When surrender and humility help one get out of the way, it ushers in the infinite realm where effortless healing and transformation happen. Even though this is a simple concept, it is rarely easy.

Chapter 12

Suicide

The soul is but a sacred circle, no beginning and no end.

—*Daniel Ryan*

Whether we are in the physical or spiritual realm, there are opportunities to learn. When we complete our lessons, we resonate with the one mind, or God, or Universal Intelligence. Any illusion of separation falls away, and we are united with the One Mind, where there is peace beyond human understanding.

Knocking on the Door

During one of my workshops, which I call sacred circles, three men who all needed energetic healing around the heart were placed in the middle. By combining them in a smaller circle within the larger group circle, it magnified the power of the healing energy coming in from the spiritual realm. One of the men, Arthur, was receiving a transdimensional healing from the spirit of his paternal grandfather.

When this was complete, I saw a mother figure next to Ken, one of the three men standing. I had the other two sit down, and told Ken that his mother's spirit was right next to him and insisted on speaking to him. He confirmed that she had passed the year before. Her name was Carol.

I placed my hand on Ken's upper back and had him observe the emotions locked in there. I could feel that Ken was imprisoned by the intense anger he harbored toward his mother. She had caused him immense pain in her passing. I instructed him to follow his breath down into his lungs and to simply notice any physical sensations. He felt a tight constriction at the base of his neck and across his upper back. As he placed his attention on this area, he could also feel the anger. I instructed Ken to simply notice the emotion without trying to fix or change it, knowing the power of our attention would illuminate the stuck emotions and free them.

He began to shake slightly. All the people in a circle around us were sending healing energy to him, some with their hands outstretched in front of them, and others with their hands on their laps, holding a healing space. The energy in the room was palpable, and I noticed my hands heating up and a tingling throughout my body as I opened the door to another dimension.

The spirit of Ken's mother, right next to him, beckoned intensely. She was trying to get through to him, communicating with me all the while. I was surprised at what she revealed.

"She's telling me that it's like she keeps *knocking on your door*, but you won't listen. She's right next to you, but she can't reach you." Ken looked down and away. "She says she's sorry, so very sorry. Wait, she's showing me she became unconscious. There are pills all around her. She took them, and that's what rendered her unconscious. She's showing me the way she died, from an overdose of pills."

There was a long pause.

"She committed suicide," I added.

As I said the words, it startled me, and a hush fell over the room. Ken nodded his head slightly in agreement, desperately trying to hold back the pain. I could feel that he wanted to sit down, but he had the courage to stay standing.

"She's stuck and needs to heal this with you. She wants me to tell you that she made a terrible mistake."

Carol asked me to look into Ken's eyes to convey the message. She insisted I repeat it several times, standing right in front of him, face to face. I felt the intensity of Ken's mother looking through my eyes and deep into her son, like a laser. She had me place my left hand over his heart and repeat the following, while the searing love she was sending through my eyes forged a path into his heart.

"I'll never leave you again. I'll never leave you again. I'll never leave you again," she insisted.

The intensity of the love I felt through my hands and eyes escalated quickly. I knew something had to give. Suddenly, an energetic explosion blew out behind Ken! It felt like a vacuum sucked all the air out of the room. Moved by the dramatic shift that had taken place, several people in the group were instantly moved to tears. Everything opened and felt light and beautiful. Like violet fireworks in the sky, the energy gradually dissipated, weightlessly trickling down.

"We need to help Carol," called a woman from the group, breaking the silence. It was Carol's turn. She had come to help her son, and now she needed help in moving on. She had been trying to reach him for so long and with all of her attention, and now she needed healing as well. Carol was stuck between worlds.

Once again, we summoned the healing power of the circle and conveyed all the love to Carol. In communication, I helped guide her toward the light—the light of resolution and Christ consciousness. I could see her spirit being filled with light and love, and suddenly she was everywhere.

After a few minutes, with only sniffles breaking the silence in the room, I gave Ken a hug and instructed the group to give him a hug as well before they left for the evening.

I'm Sorry

Looking through the large plate-glass windows of my studio, I noticed that the sky was particularly bright blue that day, a fresh canvas for the pure white billowing clouds. It was almost as if they were parachutes gently suspending inspiration from heaven. My eyes drank up the sparkle of the many diamonds dancing across the ocean, a gift from the sun. My whole being stopped, and I recognized that it was good to be alive. I took a deep breath of the astonishing life force that was all around me.

A content hum accompanied my exhale as I slowly turned my head to greet Natalie. She had come to me as a last resort to see if I could heal her energetic constriction of the past fifteen years. She was a tall, slender, athletic tennis player with the remnants of freckles sprinkled across her face, suspended in time from her childhood forty-five years earlier. Her easy smile welcomed me to the home of her heart space. Her light green and hazel eyes were a striking complement to her auburn hair delicately draping her shoulders.

The years had been kind to Natalie, filled with laughter, wisdom, and acceptance. Although her first marriage had been to a man who was just like her mother, she chose to see it as a unique learning experience. Now at fifty, after years of personal growth, she had finally allowed herself to be vulnerable enough to see and accept her soul mate, to whom she had been married for the past year and a half.

"Life is good," she told me. "If only I didn't have this blocked feeling, it would be even better."

"Let's see what we can do here," I said as I evaluated her energetically.

I held her head in the supine position while I began balancing her body energetically.

As I was working, the air in the room became dense. My eyes remained closed as the face of an older woman appeared to me. She felt like Natalie's mother. She was fair with strawberry ringlets reaching just below her ears. Her large green eyes beckoned me with concern. Even though this phenomenon happens frequently, I'm always surprised and fascinated when it occurs. I asked Natalie if she had ever felt her mother around.

"No, it's been so long since she passed. But if you do, please let me know," she responded.

"I do feel her spirit around you. Would you like to speak to her?"

"Yes, I would if she has something to say to me."

With a look of remorse, her mother spoke slowly and delicately. "I'm sorry, sweetheart."

When I conveyed what her mother said, I felt a tight feeling around my neck. I coughed between words and had trouble finishing the sentence. Immediately, Natalie's eyes poured forth the grief that she had long ago attempted to eradicate from her being. It only seemed to take a few moments for her to integrate this validation into her reality. I waited for her to continue.

"It's been ten years since that day," Natalie continued, attempting to catch her breath. "She committed suicide. . . . She hung herself. . . . That's why she's sorry."

The air left the room. I stood speechless, shocked and feeling strangely awkward after revealing what Natalie's mother had said. The ominous constriction around my neck was an unpleasant side effect of communicating with her mother's spirit. In an attempt to communicate their message accurately, spirits will sometimes give the physical feeling they experienced as they passed. Occasionally, as in this scenario, I have to tell the spirit to stop because I get the message a little too loud and clear.

Natalie turned her attention toward me, saying, "Are you okay? You look a little pale."

"What do you mean like I just saw a ghost that was trying to strangle me?" I replied.

We burst out in laughter.

"I had no idea you could do that type of thing. That's amazing. It's funny, I hadn't thought about her in so long until a few days ago," she said.

"Oftentimes, people will start thinking about the spirits that are around them. It may be your subconscious that was picking up on your mom," I explained.

"That's weird. My chest feels so light now, and, hey, my neck pain is gone. How about that?" Natalie's gratitude opened her face with a loving smile.

Then her mother had more to say. "Tell your brother, Graham, that I'm sorry for what I did and please forgive me for the way I treated Debbie as well."

Natalie smiled incredulously as I conveyed her mother's message.

"How could you know that? She never liked my brother's wife, and she hadn't spoken with them for three years before her death."

"I didn't know that until your mother told me just now."

"I'll tell him, Mommy."

Natalie's mother's energy blended with Natalie, raising both of their vibrations. A deep violet color intensified through and about them as they merged.

"I feel a strange tingle pulsing through my body," Natalie said.

"Your mother is merging her energy with yours and healing you," I said.

Natalie wept as the energetic compartmentalization of her heart was obliterated.

"When a soul sheds its mortal coil, spirits will have certain epiphanies about their life in that transition," I explained. "It appears that your mother has definitely gained a new perspective since her transition, and she has come back to help you as well. Spirits have the ability to participate in transdimensional healing, and your mother is reaching out to you in this way."

"I guess I didn't know what to think about my mom after she passed away. It was all so sudden," Natalie confided. "It was as if someone slammed a door in my face and locked it. It never occurred to me that maybe I was the one who shut the door and locked it. It makes sense that I would have to deal with it sooner or later. Thank you. Thank you so much. I know now that I've needed that healing and resolution for a long time."

We hugged, cleansed in gratitude for the experience before we parted ways for the day. I was grateful for being able to help her re-open the door. Natalie appeared different after that day, more fully present. We continued to work together in the following weeks, successfully clearing away residual stagnant energy patterns. She continued to integrate her new openness, facilitating a deeper and richer connection in all of her relationships.

Escape

War is on
My mind is fleeing
My heart is fighting
My spirit is weary
My eyes are bleeding
Peace cannot be bought
Peace can only be realized
Its presence unfolds through surrender
Blessed be those who see through the eyes of a child
Listen carefully
Spirit is speaking
Spirit is calling you
Spirit is calling me
Blessed be, we are so free!

—Daniel Ryan

Chapter 13

Family

There are only two ways to live your life.
One is as though nothing is a miracle.
The other is as though everything is a miracle.

—*Albert Einstein*

Gratitude has an opportunity to be born out of the depth of what may be a difficult experience. How are we to know how good something is if we haven't known how bad it can be? The spectrum of our experiences is relative, and the value that one places upon it defines it. A self-realized being sees things just as they are and is grateful for it all.

Behind the Iron Curtain

The hard life Faina had lived in the Soviet Union hung like steel from her face, making her appear much older than her forty-eight years. As a child, she would help her father lift heavy boxes that were delivered to the family bakery. Her day would start at 4:00 a.m. when she would begin assisting her father with the baking and cleaning at the shop. These were hard times in Russia, and most of the population was focused on mere survival. The Cold War had made its way into the hearts and stomachs of the people. Faina said she was lucky that their family had a bakery because what they produced was a viable commodity: food. Even when they didn't have proper heat, they at least had bread.

At the age of thirteen, Faina's father seriously injured his leg when an out-of-control motorcycle clipped him and sent him flying while he was delivering to a customer. Because of this tragedy, Faina had to quit school to help her father full-time and support the family. But she never let go of her dream of becoming a doctor. She endured a harsh climate, poverty, and family hardships, but through her perseverance, she prevailed and became a medical doctor specializing in ophthalmology.

During her residency, she met Dominic, a medical director at the hospital. He touched a part of her that had never been reached emotionally. They fell in love and were married within the year.

After her sister died of breast cancer, Faina eventually migrated to America, where she started a new life with her husband and son. The secret about her son would soon be revealed while communicating with the spirit of her sister.

While we were talking, I became aware of a presence in the room. I became still and opened my senses. A thick silver moustache came forth, framed by a dauntingly serious expression.

"Are you open to spiritual healing?" I asked.

"Yes, I am very open to whatever will help me."

"There is a spirit here who would like to connect with you. Are you open to that?"

Faina's eyes opened with surprise, before tripping over her words.

"Sure, I think so. Who is it?"

"I see a man in his mid-fifties with a big silver moustache. His hair is parted on the right with a high forehead. He feels like a father figure."

With an intrigued smile and a blush, Faina asked, "Can I talk to him?"

"Yes, he can hear you and would like that very much," I replied.

"My father is still alive, but that sounds exactly like Gregory, my best friend who was like a father to me in many ways."

"He's showing me that he smoked and later developed cancer in his upper chest."

"Yes, he did smoke, and he died of cancer in his chest and throat."

"He's telling me that your sister is here, and he is taking care of her now. Does this make sense to you?"

This rendered Faina speechless. Her eyes moistened as we looked at one another. Faina's whole being softened with a prodigious sigh.

"Your sister is coming forward now. She appears angry. She didn't want to go. She keeps saying that it just wasn't right."

"No, it wasn't. She was only thirty-six with a son who was two and a half," she said.

"She's telling me that you have always been the mature one, the one she leaned on. She's telling me that you're a wonderful mother and wants to thank you from the bottom of her heart for taking care of her son."

Faina's face turned red, painted with emotion. She leaned in and lowered her voice almost to a whisper as if she had a secret to tell.

"My son is really her son that my husband and I raised, but no one knows that. This is what she is talking about." A wellspring of tears came forth as the truth opened her up.

"She's showing me that she had breast cancer, and that's how she passed."

"Yes, she did have breast cancer that had metastasized from her liver, and that's what took her."

"She wants to thank you for always watching out for her like a big sister. She loves you and thinks that you're an awesome mother, and would like to give you a present."

With that, her energy morphed into Faina's, transforming the heaviness of her being into light. As they came together, their luminescent glow intensified. Faina was now overjoyed and almost giddy as she spoke.

"Wow I can feel her, she's actually my older sister, but it's true that I always took care of her like a big sister. There were times when I wasn't sure if I was doing the right thing as a mother, so I feel better now receiving validation form her about our son."

"She's telling me that there was a time when she was thinking about not having the baby, and you helped her make the decision to keep him. She's so grateful for that. Do you remember?"

Smiling through her tears, Faina said, "Yes, yes, yes, we wanted this baby so much."

"She's thankful for the way you've mothered him. You've done an amazing job. She says that she loves you and wants you to know that she is always watching over you."

"I love you, too," Faina replied.

Apparently unaccustomed to and overwhelmed by what had just transpired, she suddenly looked embarrassed by her display of emotion. After the session, I noticed that Faina's face had changed, as if a huge weight had been lifted. Her disc condition in her lower back improved dramatically after that day. The lower back represents the foundation of the spine, as well as the foundation emotionally. Thus, with the healing of her and her sister's spirits, it was no accident that her lower back improved so quickly. The mind and body are one, so whatever occurs in the mind affects the body, and vice versa.

Later, I looked up the meaning of "Faina" in Russian. It means "light." I found this to be no coincidence.

Physicians Assist

Eileen had endured her share of hard knocks in life. To mention a few, her father died of leukemia when she was only five years old, she survived lymphoma herself as a young woman, and, most recently, she had fallen on the way to the bathroom in the middle of the night and sustained a near-fatal head injury. This was a major blow to her body, as well as her psyche.

It had been just over a year since Eileen's accident when she came to me for help. She had been in a coma for three weeks after the accident when they surgically opened her skull, not knowing if she would make it. This was a tragic event for her and her husband and two pre-teenage boys. Fortunately, she had survived. Now, still plagued by neurological symptoms and post-traumatic stress syndrome, she decided to give energetic healing a try after she heard about me from a friend of her family. She had exhausted other modalities over the past year, most of which had helped only temporarily. Eileen had been the super-mom to her two adolescent boys and a devoted wife to her husband. She had also been very active in the community, especially at her sons' school. As she described her condition to me, she made it very clear that she was unwilling to accept any of her limitations as permanent. Her fortitude paradoxically compounded her anxiety because there was a part of her that still believed she would never heal. The anxiety then exacerbated her head and neck pain. I believed that I understood her condition and could help her. As we spoke, a wellspring of fear and uncertainty came forth in her eyes, forming both ponds of hope and swirling despair reflecting back at me.

I knew this was the beginning of a long healing process, and I assured her that I wouldn't quit on her. I became a reliable safe haven for Eileen to rest her head upon, which helped create a foundation for her healing. Within a few weeks of working together, Eileen began to believe that she would get better again after her physical symptoms had lessened. We both became more excited after seeing that we were on the right course. We built up a mutual trust over several weeks, which created a healing space that opened whenever we met.

One day while Eileen was having a bad day, we discussed her progress. While we were talking, I felt the presence of a spirit in the room. A tingling sensation blew right through me, commanding my attention. His face came into focus, and I noticed that he felt like Eileen's father, whom I had never met. He looked just like Eileen's brother, David, whom I had met a few times. I looked at Eileen and began to describe what I saw.

"Boy, your father looks just like your brother, David," I said.

"Yes, he does. How did you know that?"

"I'm seeing your father's spirit around you right now."

"Really?" Eileen asked.

"Yes, and he's showing me that there was something wrong with his brain, like the wires were crossed."

"Yes, he had epilepsy. He didn't want anyone to know because he was a physician, and it could affect his career."

"He's showing me that he performed surgery in the chest and heart area."

"Yes, he was a thoracic surgeon specializing in oncology. You're really connecting with him, aren't you?"

"Yes, he's coming through very clearly. His demeanor is a bit cold and to the point."

"Yes, that's exactly how he was. He was not always the nicest man, very self-centered and arrogant, but maybe he's here to help me."

"Yes, he wants to help you. That is why he's here."

The frown contracting her father's forehead was accompanied by a serious, dry tone.

"I want you to stop taking that medication," he said. "It's causing the dizziness you've been having. And I want you to see a different doctor, one who understands your condition better."

I relayed this information to Eileen.

"Which medication? I'm on a few," she asked.

"It starts with an 'm,' he's telling me."

"There's one that starts with an 'n,' but not an 'm.'"

"Yes, he says that's the right one you're thinking of."

Later, Eileen actually confirmed that the generic name for the medication did start with an "m."

"That's interesting. They were giving it to me after the fall to help with the internal tremors. I'll stop taking it."

"I have to tell you that I can't take you off any medication, so please check with your prescribing doctor first, regardless of your father's opinion," I said.

"Okay, but he was a brilliant physician, and I do trust his knowledge," Eileen said.

"Your father would like to send healing energy through you if that's all right with you."

"Yes, I welcome any help I can get, but what does that look like?"

"He can send energy from the spiritual realm to help balance you. I believe that when spirits help this way, it can actually facilitate a positive shift in your DNA. You just need to relax and be receptive, which will make it easier. In the process, I will hold your head and balance your energy while you lay on your back."

"Okay, let's do it," she said.

With my eyes closed and hands above Eileen's body, I was fascinated to see a deep indigo blue stream of light infuse her spinal cord, almost as if she became a black-and-white drawing with the nervous system colored. The indigo blue was pulsating in waves up and down her body.

Out of curiosity, I asked Eileen's father what he had died of, but he brushed me aside quickly, saying that he wanted to focus only on healing Eileen right then, and it wasn't important how he had passed. After five minutes passed, he was done, and Eileen's energy felt balanced and calm to me.

When I told Eileen about the intensity and focus of her father on helping her heal, she was very touched. She said this was significant because she had felt as a child that he was always busy and didn't give her the attention she needed.

"Tell her that I will be sending her healing energy between 2:00 and 5:00 a.m. over the next week," her father continued. I conveyed the message.

"Wow, okay. That will be fine. I'll be asleep, and I would love the help," Eileen replied.

I told her, "It helps to mention it to you so your subconscious is receptive to it during the process."

Then her face flushed, and she began to cry as she was visibly moved by her father's gesture.

"Oh, and he wants to say one more thing," I said. "'Tell David that I'm sorry for the way I treated him. I think I wounded him as a man.'"

Eileen threw her head back with an exasperated exhale.

"I know exactly what he means by that statement."

"His energy is fading now. Is there anything else you would like to ask him?"

"Tell him I love him and thank him for all his help."

After a few minutes, we discussed the significance of the session.

"My brother had problems with his ears, and had trouble playing sports and being athletic when he was younger. My father couldn't relate to him because of this and pushed him away emotionally. Consequently, they didn't have much of a relationship during that time."

"I asked your father what he died of, and he wouldn't tell me. He only wanted to focus on healing you."

"Wow, he has changed. That's so sweet that he just wanted to focus on me. That alone means so much to me. He was a brilliant man, but he was self-centered, and I know that this is his way of letting me know that he has changed. He died of leukemia from radiation exposure during the Second World

War. All of the men who were on that ship that was close to the testing site are now dead because of it," she explained. "I feel different now. I'm so touched that he wants to help me."

This session opened up new hope for Eileen. She has continued her gradual ascension from the depth of her fear and despair, and is well on the way to having "normal" aches and pains with certain activities.

A Family Secret

Johnny was elated when he entered my studio one day. He had turned twenty-six the day before and was still feeling the effects of a fantastic night out, celebrating his birthday with his friends.

Johnny had grown up in Ohio, the youngest of six boys in a Mormon family. He knew from a very young age that he was different. He had the normal crushes that other boys did, except that they weren't on girls. His family knew, but Johnny kept his feelings to himself at the risk of being ostracized from his family and conservative community, including the church. Burying this secret caused him tremendous pain and deep feelings of loneliness, and he sought me out to help him heal.

As we began our session together, I felt the depth of isolation and pain that this secret had caused Johnny, lodged in his body. Immediately, I sensed his maternal grandfather's spirit in the room. I was grateful for the assistance and guidance he provided.

Johnny had been to my workshops and was very open to the metaphysical realm, and he welcomed his grandfather to join us, even though they had never met while he was still living. Johnny's mother had always told him that he was very much like his grandfather. His mother attributed her and Johnny's closeness to the fact that she had been very close to her father, and Johnny reminded her of him.

"I know exactly how you feel, Johnny," his grandfather said. "You see, I was a lot like you, except I never told anyone. I kept it to myself all my life. I'm so proud that you had the courage to tell your family, and endure the rejection and confusion for the sake of being your Authentic Self."

Johnny shook and wept deeply as I relayed the message. It was as if he finally felt understood from someone in his family.

Johnny told me, "Throughout my body, and especially in my heart, I have felt the pain, sadness, and loneliness that my grandfather felt throughout his life. Like a flashback flipping through the life of a man I never knew, I can feel the weight of what he went through. I realize now that I wasn't alone. My grandfather suffered as I have. Now I know that my grandfather is grateful for the life I've been brave enough to lead, and is happy with the friends I've chosen to keep close. He is proud of me."

I told Johnny, "Your grandfather is talking about your aunt, your mother's older sister, Carla. He's showing her with a dark grey cloud around her head. She's very depressed. Your grandfather says that he always found it particularly difficult to connect with Carla, as did your mother. But he wants Carla to know that he loves her, and that your mother needs to continue reaching out to her."

Johnny's mother found out indirectly through family members that Carla's son had revealed to her that he was gay. She approached Carla's daughter to ask why Carla hadn't sought her support after her son had revealed this to her. Carla's daughter didn't know her brother had admitted to being gay, which set off a firestorm within the family that culminated with Carla calling Johnny's mother, irate that she had discussed their situation without her permission.

"Your grandfather is saying that Carla has often compared herself to your mother. She feels like your mother has had it so much easier. He wants Carla to know that he loves her. He is saying a name that starts with a 'Br,' like Brent."

"Yes, Carla's husband's name is Brent."

"He's showing me a log. Does that mean anything to you?"

"Yes, my grandfather built a log cabin, and the sisters are currently having a disagreement about it."

"He's showing me how he used to love to cut wood."

"Yes that's true and my grandfather even looked like me," Johnny said.

"He says that you were twin brothers in a past life and, in fact, you have been together in many lives. Two lifetimes ago, you were brothers, and your last name was Brenner. You are twin souls, and now that you have re-connected, he promises that from this moment on and for every step you take the rest of your life and beyond, he will be with you."

As his grandfather spoke, a deep indigo light streamed from him into Johnny.

"Your grandfather is sending you healing energy. He says that you have a problem with your thyroid, but with the energy he is sending, it will change the potential outcome of your genetic expression and eradicate any problems with your thyroid in the future."

"That's incredible. I've been experiencing many symptoms of having a thyroid problem. My dad has had thyroid problems all his life."

I witnessed the energetic healing as the ethereal light permeated his body. I felt a tingling shift through my body. I was receiving a blessing as well. Instantly, everything became lighter, as if Johnny had broken free of his shackles. I was done with what I was meant to do that day, but I could feel that Johnny was still cooking.

"You are still processing. Just relax, and I'll see you out front when you're finished," I said. Before he left I recommended that he consult his M.D. to evaluate his thyroid.

Later, Johnny told me that he continued to feel the presence of his grandfather after I left the room. He spoke to him, filling him up with energy while lifting the pain he had stored from years of self-hatred. Johnny finally got off the table and put on his street clothes. Unlike past sessions, this time the feeling of energy flowing into his body didn't end when he left the room. It stayed with him for hours.

We continued our conversation after Johnny emerged from the room about fifteen minutes later. Well, I should say that we sort of continued because Johnny was practically speechless and beside himself. After he gathered his thoughts, he told me a story.

Johnny shared how his mother was trying to understand the concept of gay men raising children and having families of their own. The idea of homosexuals raising children seemed absurd to her. That was, until she accompanied Johnny to his friend's house for dinner. They were an older gay couple with children. They had been blessed with twin girls who were now nine months old.

Johnny's mother's perspective completely changed when she entered their home and saw the incredible love that these parents had for their twins. Suddenly, she understood.

"Seeing them get their two babies ready for bed, feeding them their bottles, I just can't understand why anyone would be against that. They love those babies so much, and those children are so lucky to have such wonderful, loving parents."

That simple dinner quickly opened her heart. She experienced firsthand how universal a parent's love for a child is, no matter if the child has a mother and a father, or two fathers. They had the normal parental challenges and triumphs that traditional families have, and probably a few more.

Johnny's mother's perspective and awareness completely shifted, simply by witnessing the universal power of love. She now has a greater acceptance of many different types of families. "After all, we are all in this together. We may as well enjoy it and love one another," she said.

The gratitude that Johnny held for his grandfather's assistance and insights, and his mother's openness to a different lifestyle, were, in his words, "humbling and profound." The weight lifted from his face, body and whole being.

Chapter 14

Energetic Healing

Sit down before fact like a little child,
and be prepared to give up every preconceived notion.
Follow humbly wherever and to whatever
abyss Nature leads, or you shall learn nothing.

—*Thomas H. Huxley*

Everything is energy. It has been proven scientifically that there is no such thing as a neutral observer. We influence, and are influenced, by our environment. Energy exchange is constant. This is why one of the best ways to help others heal is by healing oneself. This makes you a clear channel to assist others in their transformations. We can only help others to the degree that we have helped ourselves. Otherwise, we may be reinforcing existing limited patterns in others by resonating at the same limited energetic frequency. Sally, a challenging case study, gave me an opportunity to practice this principle.

The Body Remembers

Excited by the opportunity to help someone who was obviously in dire need of assistance, I graciously welcomed Sally in for a session. I fought back the shock clearly displayed on my face when I discovered Sally's age. The deep furrows of her skin weathered her well beyond her years. Her light hazel eyes told a story of desperation. Standing 5'2" and thin as a twig, she looked as though she could be snapped in two with an unkind word. A very sensitive and intelligent woman, she proceeded to recite volumes of stories and medical diagnoses that she had accumulated from the doctors she had seen over her sixty years.

Hemochromatosis was the answer the doctors finally gave her after years of tests, a hysterectomy, two hip replacements, and a shoulder replacement. Hemochromatosis is a physiological condition in which the body accumulates excess iron that wrecks havoc throughout all the body's systems. I asked what she hoped to gain from our session together. As she gave me a view of her innermost secrets, the mask of her history abruptly fell away like a window being shattered. She pleaded for any help that I could provide her, including intuitive healing in addition to the medical treatment that she was receiving.

As I listened to Sally describe her life condition, I very clearly saw the spirit of her father standing over her right shoulder and a younger male spirit next to her left shoulder that felt like her brother. Her father began to speak to me.

"Your father passed away some time ago, in the '70s, right?"

"Yes, how did you know?"

"I see his spirit. He's standing next to you, and he's talking to me."

Her face fell forward into her hands. She slowly lifted her head after a few moments.

"Can I talk to him? He's actually my adopted father."

"Yes, he's a very kind spirit, and I can see how close you two were. He says he's here to help with your healing process if that's okay with you."

"Yes, yes, please."

"Your father is showing me that he is predominantly here to help you heal. He says he can do this by providing energy that is not limited to our physical laws. His energy is very quiet and focused on assisting you with selfless intention."

I attempted to obtain more information from him, but he redirected me.

I'm grateful that I was open and able to help facilitate the phenomenon that occurred next. I laid my hands upon Sally's upper back while she lay face down. Images began to flow through my mind's eye until they hit the cold, concrete dam concealing a trauma of long ago. She had been raped when she was eighteen by three young men. Also, she had been with another girl at the time, who had left her there and didn't help.

Sally had held all of these people in contempt for the past forty-two years. As I witnessed this revelation, the tears from her eyes looked as though they were poured directly form her heart. Sally's astounded face met mine, vulnerable and open.

"That's exactly right. I can't believe that's coming up now, it was so long ago."

"The body never forgets and will harbor the pain until it is released. By illuminating these stagnant cellular memories, they dissipate from the body," I said. "Your father is giving me another message. He is showing me that he died of a heart attack."

"Yes, he was only forty-three, so young."

What I witnessed next amazed me. Her father started sending energy to her. It swirled down into her like a funnel. As it penetrated her body, it split into five horizontal planes, each about two inches apart. The planes formed a grid formation and then began connecting to one another in various places, as if the energy was arching and creating synaptic junctures. On a more superficial level, he was continuing to send Sally messages, as if to distract her surface mind while he was doing the real healing.

Sally's eyes began darting frantically side to side, as if she were a terrified, caged bird seeking to escape. Then, as quickly as it started, it subsided, as if something bigger than herself had slapped her out of the frenzy. She looked as though she had suddenly woken up. Her eyes bugged out and propelled her into a vast horizon of clarity. Visibly shaken but steadfast with new determination, she urged me to continue. "The other young man that feels like your brother says that you can find your biological family in Arkansas, under the name of Byers."

She looked at me incredulously.

"I don't know. I was adopted. I was conceived out of an affair and put up for adoption. My father apparently had a large family already. I don't know if I have a brother or not, but why would I want to find my biological father anyway? He didn't want me."

"This information could have greater importance to you at a later date. You may want to write it down," I said.

As the session came to a close, Sally's contorted face revealed the transmutation of many belief systems as she tried to make sense of what just happened.

"How are you feeling, Sally?" I asked.

"Wow, I had no idea, but I sure didn't expect that!"

Sally's breath began to slow to a new rhythm, one suited for a more peaceful place. It was of the kind of peace you experience through a direct knowing that is greater than oneself.

I asked Sally's father about the significance of the energy grids. He told me that spirits have the ability to gather energy and transfer it into the physical realm. This action transmutates the DNA, affecting the genetic expression of disease and dysfunction. In other words, it can actually change the outcome of current conditions and can be preventative for future illnesses. I had witnessed this before, but this was the first time it had been explained in such explicit detail. This was very exciting, I began to understand the origin of what I had been facilitating for so many years, and the possibilities were limitless.

Over the next week, Sally came into see me for two more sessions.

"The body reveals the levels that need to be healed when it's ready, like peeling layers from an onion," I explained.

One time, she came in feeling constricted. . As I laid my hands on the area, I immediately felt that she had an opportunity to release the sadness and anger she harbored toward her mother.

"What's causing the pain?" she asked.

"Your mother," I replied.

A gasp traveled from deep within her, and sadness for her mother expelled from her body. Sally's surprise caused her to lift her head off the table. With her eyes shining like headlights, she squeaked out, "You got to be kidding me."

Still amazed at what her body continued to reveal, she gave herself a few breaths. She eventually calmed down and collected her thoughts before leaving that day.

The next time I saw her, a more content energy relaxed her face, and she was ready to accept the next level, I could feel the demise of her relationship with her husband due to her inability to see him emotionally. I could feel the vast sea of projection emanating from her stagnant negative cellular memories blinding her to the present moment.

"When are you going to forgive your husband?" I asked.

Spontaneous laughter exploded from her as she lit up with hope. Sally no longer appeared to be surprised by what I felt from her body.

"Do you really think I can?"

"Yes, of course you can. You have new eyes now."

We shared a hug of humble gratitude before she left. A couple of months later, I spoke with Sally again, and she was ecstatic with the results of her recent blood test, which indicated that the iron in her blood was normalizing.

Sally again returned and as she lay face down on the table, I remained open to what would be revealed next. It was as if someone was knocking on my door. As I opened it, I very clearly saw a man with a round face, thick black hair, and a kind smile. He told me that he was deeply bonded to Sally, that they would have been married if he hadn't become ill and pushed her away.

"There's a spirit here, and he says that he used to be in a relationship with you before you were married, a long time ago."

"I had two serious relationships before I married," she muttered.

"He says that you were together right before you were married. He's trying to tell me a name. It starts with a 'J' like a 'John' sound."

"That's John. I can't believe he's here."

"He says that he loves you very, very deeply and, in fact, that you two are soul mates."

"I think we were. I mean, I know we were."

"I'm seeing that he had cancer in his left lung."

"Yes, that was just one of the many physical problems he died of."

"He says that you weren't ready for him."

"He pushed me away. He said that he didn't want to burden me with the responsibility of taking care of him."

"He regrets that because you two could have been together

while he was still here. I can re-connect you two energetically, and he can assist in your healing. Is that okay?"

"Yes, I would love that."

I proceeded to re-connect the energetic silver cord that connects us to the ones we love. Sally appeared to be completely humbled at this point and just shook her head in amazement and joy at all that had transpired.

Later, she shared with me that she sees her husband differently now. The anger is subsiding, and they even like to spend time together. On a subsequent visit, she shared with me the experience she had after her last session when the spirit of her soul mate came to visit.

"I went to the beach, and I was awestruck at the beauty of the ocean. The waves seemed to wrap around me. John was the ocean."

All this time, Sally had been sending her body mixed messages that were prohibiting the healing process. The body, as well as the Universe, will respond to precisely what we intend it to do. This will happen whether the intention is conscious or unconscious, so we must be accurate and conscious of what we wish for because we will create it. We learned together the importance of bringing the soul's intention into alignment with the conscious thought process. This was the only way for Sally to manifest her true desires. That day, Sally decided that she would choose to live.

Chapter 15

Remote Healing

*Whatever books you may read, you cannot realize
the Divine merely by intellectual effort. One must
put it into practice. That sense of oneness
can only be promoted by the practice of love
and not by any other means.*

—*Sri Sathya Sai Baba*

Remote healing is the transference of love via the realization of oneness. Healing energy emanates from the heart, pure and unconditional, and is a portal to the infinite realm. Love is infinite in its capacity to transform, reveal and heal. By merging one's aura with another, you are tapping into the One Mind, where all things are possible.

Magic

Early morning broke as the sunlight pierced the sky's darkness. My consciousness began to stir from a quasi-dream state. I could feel my friend Pat's energy constriction. He was in Colorado at the time. I originally met him years ago while he was producing an album for a prominent music artist. He had a reputation for being one of the foremost music producers in the world, with many hit songs under his belt.

When he experienced this constriction energetically it would dramatically inhibit his ability to work. I would balance the energy and it would free him up again. One time when I was leaving his music studio, I stopped to use the bathroom. On my way out, I overheard him speaking to his colleagues about me in an incredulous tone, "I don't know exactly what he does, but it's amazing how it works. It's like magic." Even though he couldn't explain what he was feeling, he felt my energy assessing the status of his being beyond the superficial realm. Pat's sensitivity always served him well with music, and I'm sure it contributed to much of his success.

As I lay in bed feeling Pat's constriction in my own body, I had the thought that I must help him. That's when my mind objected, "You can't do that because he's in Colorado."

Then I heard a reply from a place beyond the finite mind. "He's not over there. There is no 'over there.' He's right here."

I visualized balancing the energy and let it go.

My curiosity woke me fully, and I sat up smiling, excited to see if it had really worked. I waited until a decent hour to call. When Pat answered, I asked him how he was doing.

He said, "You know I was in such a horrible place last night while I was trying to do a mix, but this morning I feel fantastic." I explained to him what I had experienced that morning, and he laughed out loud, saying, "That's amazing. Hey, how do you charge for something like that?"

I decided to try this process on myself over the next few weeks. I would lay flat on my back and close my eyes, take a few deep breaths, and bring my attention to areas of my body that felt uncomfortable. I envisioned the energy being balanced and releasing all tension. Regardless of the position or what I perceived the problem to be, I visualized it being balanced and trusted that it was done. It worked! What freedom I had obtained! I had read of cancer patients that shrunk or completely eradicated tumors by using similar visualizations. Wherever I was, I could help myself without the need to go to someone else to fix it. When and how did we forget that we have the innate healing capacity to help ourselves, and others?

I became very excited at the prospect of teaching this to others, which I explain in greater detail in Chapter 19, "Healing the Healer." This is a demonstration of how effective it is to usher in oneness from the infinite realm, where the constraints of the logical mind don't exist. In this realm, things just are, and they are not limited to the definitions placed upon them. However, circumventing the logical mind or quieting it enough to hear your natural intuition from the infinite realm is a different story. Easier said than done. It can take much dedication and practice. But when it does happen, this is when magic occurs, which is our natural birthright.

Sea Captain

At 8:15 on a Saturday morning, I was walking around the house with our four-month-old baby, attempting to help my wife get some sleep since she had been up since the 5:00 a.m. feeding. The phone rang, and it was our friend, Andrea, calling to tell me that her husband, Richard, was having a hard time. I had worked on Andrea remotely before with great success, and they wanted to see if I could help Richard in the same way.

Once Richard got on the phone, I immediately sensed a spirit trying to come through to speak with him. The spirit had a long face, a moustache, and a navy blue sea captain's hat. He seemed very excited to make contact, and his energy was coming through clearly. I informed him that he would have to wait until I finished balancing Richard, and then I would see what he had to say.

I should note that I have known Richard and Andrea for many years. They knew by then that I was very open when it came to spirituality, so I could tell them anything, and often did.

"There's a spirit around you," I told Richard. "He has a long face, moustache, and a navy blue seaman's cap on."

"That's Skip," he blurted out enthusiastically. "Did I ever tell you about my grandfather? He was a sea captain in the British Guard."

"No, you never did, but that's cool," I replied.

"I don't remember him having a moustache, but I think he did when he was younger."

"Yes, he's showing me that he was about forty-five years old, and he's holding a picture of himself and your dad. Your dad was just a boy."

"Yes, I have that picture, and I was just looking at it yesterday. Wow, that's incredible."

Suddenly, I could hear Richard sniffling on the other end.

"Your grandfather says that you've been worried about your mortality lately."

Richard was turning fifty-five the next month.

"Yes, I have been," admitted Richard, in a soft, somber tone. "I want to live a long time, so I can be here for my girls."

Richard has two daughters with his wonderful wife, Andrea, who were six months old and five years old at the time.

"Your grandfather says there was a time when he was afraid he was going to die, and he shut down and pushed his wife and son away. It lasted for about six years until he was able to overcome the fear. He continued to live for a long time after that. He wants to help you avoid doing the same thing so you don't miss out on this precious time."

"He did push his family away, and I know my father was devastated by that."

"He is trying to tell me a 'J' or a 'G' sounding name," I said.

"Oh, yes. My father's name was George, even though they always called him Peter. But I'm the only one who knew that. That's amazing."

"Your father and grandfather are together and continuing to heal their relationship, even though your dad is still having trouble trusting him."

"Yeah, I know my dad felt that way. He was really hurt by his dad."

"They want you to know that the legacy of men in the family is with you, even when you think you're all alone in this world."

A prodigious sigh came through the receiver, as though some weight had been lifted from Richard's shoulders. I could feel his energy being very still in contemplation.

"That's amazing. I didn't expect that. Who would have known that he would still be around to help me out?"

As I relayed the messages, I witnessed a wave of energy warping my field of vision. A funnel of indigo light infused Richard's heart, making it appear a luminescent white.

"Your grandfather is sending you healing energy. You may feel a tingling sensation throughout your body. It's best if you continue to relax and stay open to the experience."

I knew that a dramatic energetic shift was taking place, eradicating the fear. This change would forever alter Richard's perception and open his heart again to the present moment. I suspected that his impending mortality weighed heavily upon his being, as his love for his family had grown. This, of course, is ultimately what each and every human being must face, be it conscious or unconscious. I have noticed a recurring theme with spirits who have crossed over, only to be surprised that their souls continue on—and that they had not escaped dealing with their unresolved issues simply by dying.

It was a blessing for Richard to have his grandfather come through and convey his wisdom from his own experience. I have seen this occur frequently, as the spirit world is always attempting to help us expand consciously.

Three Generations

"Who is it you would like to talk to, Matt?" I asked.

"My father. We referred to him as Grampa Bo since Jeremy, my son, was born three years ago, and I would also like to speak to my wife's parents as well." Juliana's parents had come through on a few other occasions for her.

"I have a couple of other things that I thought you could help me with."

I had sessions with the whole family before. Jeremy, their three-year-old, is extremely intuitive and empathic. He was feeling emotions from other people and not processing them through his body very well. Consequently, he would get pain and discomfort in his solar plexus, located just below the navel. Jeremy's struggles reminded me of the challenges I had as a child, so I really wanted to teach him a few things about his gift.

As a child, I didn't realize that much of what I was feeling was coming from other people. It took many years of reflection to fully understand how to empower myself with my sensitivity instead of being a victim, resistive and reactive to it. Now, Jeremy and his mother Juliana were in Seattle, Matt was with me in Los Angeles, and Grampa Bo was in another dimension.

Grampa Bo had passed away a year and a half prior. I had facilitated remote, or long-distance, healing before, but never like this. I didn't know if the spirit of Matt's father would be available, but fortunately he was. In addition they asked if I could help Juliana as well. She was seven months pregnant with their second child, who had just turned breach the week before and was being monitored closely by her doctor but wanted some energy balancing as well.

"Is that all? No pressure?" I joked.

I focused my attention to see if Grampa Bo was around. I did feel him, but he wouldn't show himself to me at first. He seemed resistant for some reason. Finally, he showed me only his beautiful light blue eyes. I was a bit surprised because Matt, with his dark brown eyes and hair, didn't resemble him in his coloring.

I told Matt about his father's eyes, and he said, "That's exactly right. They actually have a painting in the living room at home of Grampa Bo that accentuates his striking blue eyes." Matt became very excited after I described this physical detail of his father.

Grampa Bo then said, "Your mother has a beautiful heart," while showing me a pristine white pulsating heart, a symbolic representation of the purity of her intention. "And I'm sorry about what happened with your mother."

Matt nodded as though he understood, and I felt that what he was referring to wasn't for me to know, so I respectfully didn't ask.

"How can I have a better relationship with Aunt Sharon, your sister?" Matt asked.

"She has never been interested in staying close to the family, so if you approach her about the family, she won't be interested," Grampa Bo replied. "If you want to connect with her, talk to her about a mutual interest, and she will perk right up."

"And what can I do about my brother-in-law and all the trouble he's been causing?"

"He's very egocentric at this time in his evolvement. If he wants to treat the family this way, then you kids need to take care of each other and treat this like a business deal. Matt, you will have to be the one to handle it with Michael. Don't bother Juliana with this anymore. It's causing her too much stress."

Matt again mentioned his concern about Juliana's baby being breach. I tuned into her up in Seattle and visualized the baby and balanced her energetically. I saw that Juliana was going to have a little girl, which Jeremy had confidently predicted just the week before. Then I sent energy remotely to Jeremy. I shifted the energy in his back and solar plexus to balance him while Matt and Grampa Bo helped. At one point, Grampa Bo told me to tell Matt that he was trying too hard, which was actually blocking the energy. He encouraged him to please just try to relax! We all shared a good laugh.

This fantastic experience reminded me that we are only bound by the limitations of our belief systems. As this was the first time I had facilitated a three-way healing, I felt grateful that I was open enough to get out of the way of myself to allow this phenomenon to take place.

We called Juliana and Jeremy after we finished the session, and Jeremy already felt much better. We let Juliana know that she wasn't going to need to help with the situation with her brother anymore because Matt would handle it with Michael. She exhaled a huge sigh of relief as she said, "Thank you!"

Three weeks later, at the next ultrasound appointment, Matt and Juliana were excited to discover that they indeed were going to have a baby girl, and she was now in the correct position and right on track with her development. We all shared in the blessing.

The Season of Seeing and Being Seen

I see you again through the barren landscape.
Wind of the eternal fire whips my consciousness.
Standing tall the infinite holds you.
Unwavering knowing burns through,
Narrowly escaping the hostile terrain of my psyche.
Gone is this space inside my skin that is hard as steel,
Cold as ice and impervious to the sun.
Resolute in intention my spirit perceives you.
I see there is no over there.
How beautiful you are, you smile upon me.
A wave of love spills over, my heart breaks free
The perils of winter fall away
We welcome the season of seeing and being seen

—Daniel Ryan

PART III

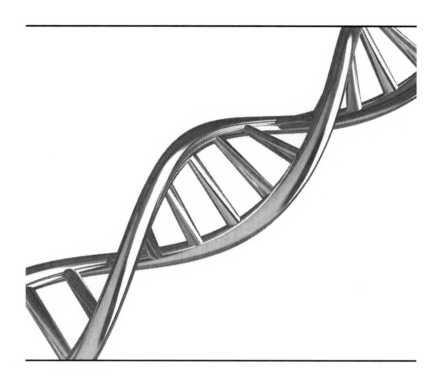

HEALING YOURSELF

Chapter 16

Journey Through Grief

The flower of one's incarnation will wilt and wither away,
but the seed of the soul is eternal.

—*Daniel Ryan*

How does one navigate through the journey of grief? Can we ever re-connect with a lost loved one? Are the memories of them enough? Beyond receiving a message from a lost loved one, what else can be done to help navigate our way through loss? Does it help to hold onto the material things they once possessed? If we believe there is life after death, does it make losing a loved one any easier?

These are difficult questions that do not have definitive answers because each individual's process of healing varies. But there are similarities between people's healing process and common knowledge we can draw upon to guide us through healing grief.

When you are grieving, the mind attempts to distract you and create defense mechanisms to bury emotions that cause stagnant energetic patterns in the body. In Chapter 19, "Healing the Healer," I describe in extensive detail how to integrate and process cellular memories that have formed stagnant energetic patterns. As you tune into these feelings, and observe and feel them, the trapped energy will disintegrate and free up your life force. These patterns may be the residue of difficult current or past life experiences, including, but not limited to, the loss of a loved one.

The symptoms of grieving may vary and may include insomnia, depression, anger, irritability, fear, anxiety, chest pain, and even thoughts of suicide. Grieving is a very normal and natural part of the healing process. As this process takes over and turns one inside out, things no longer make any sense the way they did before. There are very normal cycles to grieving as the healing process unfolds. Although this book deals with the loss of a loved one, these stages also apply to the loss of a job or house or any other significant part of your identity.

The news of a lost loved one can be shocking and leave you feeling paralyzed with an inability to achieve simple tasks. This dazed feeling may last for a few hours or several days or longer. It's important to have a good support group around you. This helps you process the feelings because when the initial shock wears off, a wave of pain and emotion may hit you. This will pass in time, and life will return to somewhat normal circumstances again, but at the time this thought may seem impossible and unbearable.

The following stages are natural and normal with loss:

1. **DENIAL:** "I feel fine." "This can't be happening, not to me."

Denial is usually just a temporary defense. This feeling is generally replaced with a heightened awareness of situations and individuals who have been left behind after death.

2. **ANGER:** "Why me?" "It's not fair. How could he leave me?" "How can this happen to me?" "Who is to blame?"

In this second stage, the individual recognizes that denial cannot continue. Because of anger, the person is very difficult to care for due to misplaced feelings of rage and blame. Anyone who symbolizes life or energy is subject to projected resentment and jealousy.

3. **BARGAINING:** "Just let me have her back." "I'll do anything for a few more years with him." "I will give my life savings if . . ."

The third stage involves the hope that the individual can somehow postpone or delay death. Usually, the negotiation for an extended life is made with a higher power in exchange for a reformed lifestyle. Psychologically, the person is saying, "I understand that they will die or have died, but if I could just have more time with them to . . ."

4. **DEPRESSION:** "I'm so sad. Why bother with anything?" "I'm going to die . . . What's the point?" "I miss my loved one. Why go on?"

During the fourth stage, the person left behind begins to understand the certainty of death. Because of this, the individual may become silent, refuse visitors, and/or spend much of the time crying and grieving. This process allows the grieving person to disconnect from feelings of love and affection. It is not recommended to attempt to cheer up someone who is in this stage. It is an important time for grieving that must be processed.

5. **ACCEPTANCE:** "It's going to be okay." "I can't fight it, so I may as well accept it."

This final stage comes with peace and understanding of the death or loss. Once this stage occurs, we are able to bring back some balance in our lives.

A recurring theme I hear from spirits is how they would like to be remembered. They want to be thought of not so much as a memory, but as if they were still alive, because they are. They just don't currently have a physical body. Oftentimes, they will convey how free, light, and unbound they are from the physical limitations of the body they once inhabited, especially if they had a disability during their lifetime. They wish to be remembered as their free and light selves, not the selves bound within their physical bodies. How we remember them affects them in a negative or positive way.

Healing grief is not a linear process, but a spherical one. There will be setbacks. It reveals itself again and again as you expand to new levels of consciousness. As this occurs, you may re-experience a pain or memory of something that you thought had healed long ago. As your consciousness expands, you integrate and process things with more depth and profundity. You may be walking down the street, and a smell or something someone says may remind you of your lost loved one. The feelings that come up can knock you for a loop because you thought you were past feeling that way.

The following are warning signs of potential setbacks in the grieving process:

1. **ADDICTION:** At first, a person may feel the need to use medication to help them through the process, but this should be monitored closely by a physician and eliminated as quickly as possible so that the person does not become dependent upon the medication. Other forms of addiction may occur as a form of distraction from the pain.

2. **SUICIDAL THOUGHTS:** A person may lose all motivation and even entertain thoughts of suicide. If this persists, intervention is strongly recommended, especially if the person expresses the actual means of how they would achieve this.

3. **ISOLATION:** Any persistent behavior, such as extended periods of isolation or depression, is a sign that it's time to seek out professional grief counseling.

We are complex spiritual and emotional beings who are having human experiences. Sometimes life is messy with a thousand shades of grey. This realization is humbling. Humility is the vehicle for the divine insight that allows us to begin again, when all things are possible. People can step out of what they think they know and be with what actually is, in this moment.

When we are fully present, regrets of the past, or anxiety about something that has yet to happen do not plague us. This is not to say that it is ever easy just to sit with the pain, but the depth of the experience will be transformative, and birth new understandings and perceptions.

When we are in the depth of an emotion like grief, the pain may feel permanent and pervasive. But emotions are limited, and you will feel different over time. Things are always changing because everything is energy. Being non-judgmental and kind to yourself can be very helpful. The purpose of this learning experience will be revealed in time. The wisdom gained will be a service to others going through a similar experience in the future.

Realistic momentum helps us move forward. It doesn't mean that we approve of the loss, but we accept it. Rejuvenation will occur, and grieving is a wonderful time for reassessment. You have an opportunity to create and manifest your life from a new beginning, where you get to decide how and what direction you wish to take. This is a perfect time to become active in a support group and try new activities or adventures that you have always wanted to experience. Most of all, remember that we're all in this together. Don't be afraid to ask for help.

The Power of Grief

Julie had flown in from another part of the state for our appointment together. She looked as though a wave of sunshine had washed over her. Her golden blonde hair was parted to the side and styled forward to the shape of her jaw. She had smiling blue eyes and beautiful white teeth. Externally, she was a happy woman, eager to learn and grow. I felt uncomfortable around her, though. Something didn't match, and her energy felt cloudy. As always, I was excited to see why she came to see me.

She had fallen down a flight of stairs a year prior and had continued to get worse, even though she had been under a doctor's treatment. Her good friends, who were clients of mine, convinced her to take time away from her busy schedule as a professor to come to me for a session. At that first appointment, I realized why I was getting a cloudy feeling from her. She had been great at giving in her life, but not such a good receiver—to the point of being co-dependent. This pattern often manifests some type of physical illness eventually. As a professional, and a very committed wife and mother of two, Julie was always on the go, taking care of other people and ignoring her own health. This was not apparent to her until the insistent message that her back had been sending over thirteen months—slow down, take care of yourself, let go of unimportant things, and be open to receiving as well as giving.

I felt the spirit of her father around her, but I didn't make
it the focus of our session because there was so much to balance in her body energetically. Julie felt much better when she
left, but called the next day to find out why she was so sore
everywhere. I explained that our bodies have an incredible
capacity to adapt and compensate, which is exactly what her
body had done since her fall. When I balanced her body I
explained that it can take a day or two for the body to get used
to it due to the compensations it has made.

Over several sessions, there were more shifts, more
progress. But it was not physical. As Julie's physical condition
stabilized, an opening occurred for the many "non-physical"
aspects of her life.

During a session one afternoon, I again sensed Julie's father
in the room, and this time I mentioned it to her. He was a man
with big, loving hands, big enough to hold her with unconditional love. As he talked, I witnessed her father sending transcendental love to her, and it blew her heart charka wide open.
Julie's father was no stranger to healing. He had committed
his life to healing others as a physician. "My daddy always told
me that the most important tool he had in the office was his
box of Kleenex," Julie told me.

She lay down on the table to process all of this for a long
time as her father continued to send her lucent violet cosmic
healing energy from the spiritual realm. As the healing energy
entered her being, everything relaxed. Her energy field quickened and became much lighter. It was beautiful to witness.
Julie thanked me again and again, but I reminded her that I
didn't give her anything. It all came from within her; I only
helped reveal it.

One day, near the end of an appointment, I noticed my
hand gravitate to her right shoulder as I helped her up from
the table. Immediately, I could feel she was holding grief there,
but it didn't occur to her what it could be. She telephoned me
on her way home when its significance dawned on her.

Twenty years ago, she had delivered identical twin girls.
Emily was healthy, but Anna was stillborn. When she held both
of them for the last time, in order to have a photo of them
together, she held Anna in her right arm. The cellular memory
of that pain had been with her for two decades and was just

being revealed on a conscious level. Because she also had a healthy baby and a four-year-old daughter at the time, she never really had the time to grieve fully. My seemingly random comment brought a torment of tears and release.

Before heading to an appointment with me several months later, Julie had coffee with a friend, spending about an hour mostly talking about his mother, who had died two years before. Julie's mother had been dead for thirty-four years. When Julie arrived for her session, she was nauseous and had a sharp pain in her solar plexus, radiating toward her heart. After assessing that it wasn't an emergency I asked what she had been talking about over coffee. She said that in reminiscing about her mother, she realized how much alike they were—putting their families before their own health, always giving to others, and making sure every problem was solved and every person was happy. When her mother died at age fifty-six, Julie had assumed her care-giving role.

In sharing this story, the enormity of her loss hit her, and she burst into tears relieving the pain from her solar plexus. She could not stop crying. I explained that this, too, was grief that had not been fully expressed, and that she had been carrying it in her body as well as in her spirit. She expressed her gratitude at being in a safe and understanding environment, where she could heal so much more than the physical symptoms she had presented with so many months before.

Julie continued to be surprised by the depth of her catharsis over those few months and became more committed than ever to becoming the greatest expression of her potentiality. She continued to experience the expansion of her consciousness and the power of the healing process.

Freedom

Ominous water flow lucid to the naked eye
Seeping out of the shadows
Paradoxically the fear drawing them nearer
Demanding surrender to reveal the true essence of freedom
Reckless abandon explodes in a freefall of humility
Ever so gently becoming weightless and timeless
The enigma of the vacant tenements of one's heart
Echoing for deliverance from a nomad existence

—Daniel Ryan

Chapter 17

Contacting Loved Ones

*Spiritual liberation results from discovering
and expressing the intrinsic qualities of
enlightened consciousness that have been ours
since the moment we came into existence.*

—*Michael Bernard Beckwith*

Spirits are not seen with the five senses. But just because you do not see them does not mean that they are not there. To help people integrate the phenomenon of spirit communication, I explain that spirits are in the room but they just no longer have a physical body. You can feel and communicate with them via your intuition or higher self as another person in the conversation. We are spiritual beings with a vast soul having a human experience. Our human incarnation is only a small aspect or expression of our greater soul. Even when a soul has reincarnated, it never loses its connection with the One Mind even though it may not be aware of it. Consequently that aspect of the soul's personality can still connect with the loved ones they left behind.

A medium is one who is able to communicate with the spiritual realm through psychic phenomena. A medium can be physical or mental. Some mediums can communicate with a person who is still living in a physical body. Their higher self can contact another's higher self, and resolve issues that may be impossible to approach on the level of the personality. This is similar to communicating with those who have passed into the spiritual realm. As a medium, I communicate with the spiritual realm using different intuitive abilities. Some of these abilities are:

CLAIRSENTIENCE: This is the most common form of mediumship. It is when you sense and feel energetically the emotional state and personality of the spirit.

CLAIRVOYANCE: This is when the medium sees different images, symbols, and pictures in the mind's eye.

CLAIRAUDIENCE: The medium hears spirit voices or sound bites, and the medium also hears the thoughts that the spirit is thinking telepathically.

Physical mediums allow their bodies to be conduits for transferring the energy of the spirit into the physical realm. They use some of these techniques:

TRANCE OR TRANCE CHANNEL: When the medium goes into a trance, the spirit takes over the medium's body to convey messages.

MATERIALIZATION: Under certain conditions, the spirit draws an ethereal substance called ectoplasm out of the medium and others in the room and manipulates it so the spirit takes on a physical form.

DIRECT-VOICE: This occurs when the spirit again draws out the ectoplasm and forms an artificial voice box, which creates a human voice.

APPORTS: Solid objects can materialize through the medium. Spirits will make flowers, necklaces, coins, and other objects appear out of thin air.

AUTOMATIC WRITING: Spirits can blend their energy with the medium's to write messages. Often, the spirit's own penmanship will come through.

Mediums must raise their vibration and focus to interpret messages from spirits, which may vary from symbols to a kinesthetic feeling to direct telepathic communication. It's much like speaking to a person who's in the room except for the fact that they don't have a physical body. I use the analogy of tuning a radio to the right station: the signal becomes stronger and more vivid with very slight adjustments.

I have had to learn through trial and error not to let my mind fill in the picture or try to interpret the message based on my previous experience. In the beginning, it takes practice to be able to decipher what the spirit says and what your mind is attempting to fill in to complete the picture. If you allow your mind to participate, the mental focus will close down the connection with the spirit. The messages are much more accurate when the medium dismisses the mind to allow an opening to an altered state where the message can come through in a literal fashion. That is, the message will be more authentic in tone, verbiage, movement, rhythm, mannerisms, etc.

I have often found that people want to believe in the spiritual realm, but because of the ramifications of how it may affect their belief systems, they stop trying to believe, or their own barriers stop them. Most of the time, though, when people are presented with indisputable evidence of the spiritual realm, an energetic opening occurs and allows for a new perspective. Circumventing your belief systems and allowing yourself to be open to new possibilities is sometimes more difficult that it sounds. It's simple, but not necessarily easy. I tell people to leave their expectations at the door because the message is always perfect, even if it doesn't make sense at the time. Spirits will orchestrate validation in a way that will often be more significant than what you expect.

In theory, there are certain things that will help expedite intuitive development, but all the effort may just be keeping you busy while you naturally develop, regardless of what you do. The mind will attempt to make it appear to be a linear progression, but it's not. I once had a spiritual teacher tell me that whether I meditated or not didn't really matter. This struck me as an odd thing for him to say, and it actually rubbed me the wrong way. Over the following few days, it irritated me more and more, until I finally realized that it was the perfect message for me to hear through this teacher.

You see, I had been meditating for years, and I had built up certain expectations and beliefs around my practice, such as the amount of time necessary, the location where it would take place, and so on. With this epiphany, I began again. I let go of results and expectations, and I just sat and became still and meditated. Ironically, when I let all of this go, my intuitive guidance and direction expanded effortlessly. This also greatly assists one in communicating with the spiritual realm.

We have an innate capacity to communicate with the spiritual realm, provided we can get out of the way to allow it to happen. Having said that, there are some fundamental things one can do to enhance innate abilities to communicate with the spiritual realm.

INTENTION: I believe the most powerful way to enhance your ability to communicate is through setting a clear intention. Once you set your intention to evolve, you will. As you evolve, some of the things that once drew you to be interested in your spiritual practice will fall away. There is only one power, one presence, and one spirit. Practice is the vehicle that will transport you into remembering this. It is beyond the rational thought process of the finite mind. This cannot be figured out, but faith will reveal it to you when you are ready.

MEDITATION: Volumes of literature have been written about meditation, and I encourage you to explore the technique that inspires you the most. The important thing to remember is to keep it simple. Too many conditions and rules for your meditation will confine and limit your practice. One method to consider is the one that the Buddha practiced, *Vipassina*, which means to see things as they really are. It is one of India's most ancient techniques of meditation. It was taught in India more than 2,500 years ago as a universal remedy for universal ills.

During *Vipassana*, you simply sit in a comfortable position, close your eyes, and watch your breath. When thoughts come up (and they will), simply divert your attention back to your breath. There should be no judgment about how much or how long your focus was on something else. The thing to remember is that meditation is a tool to help quiet your mind's chatter so you can be open to your natural intuitive guidance.

THE BODY TEMPLE: You are a spiritual being having a human experience. At some point, your physical body will cease to exist, but your soul will continue on. Our physical bodies have limitations, but there are opportunities to enhance and maximize our genetics. Diet, exercise, adequate sleep, and decreasing stress levels can make it more pleasurable to be in your body and less of a distraction for you on your spiritual path. The body is like a barometer that interprets information constantly, and there are ways to optimize your barometer by supporting it properly. I encourage you to explore what works well with your body.

Food has a dramatic effect on the body's capacity to function at its optimum level. The more balanced and pure the food, the better you will feel, and the less distracted by mood swings and other negative side effects. When I've suggested that clients go on cleanses, they are often amazed at how much more stable and sane they feel.

Here are some healthy reminders:

- Exercise is vital in enhancing all of your physiological systems and provides a healthy outlet for stress.
- Sleep allows the body time to rejuvenate. It's been proven that sleep deprivation can break down all the body's functions, alter the brain's chemistry, and induce a state of insanity. Don't go crazy. Get some sleep.
- Mental balance is also imperative to achieving a healthy lifestyle. Balancing work and play with individual, one-on-one, and group activities facilitates mental balance. By implementing these ideas, it will naturally bring more balance into your life, decrease your stress levels, and allow you to be a greater conduit to the spiritual realm.

VISUALIZATION: This simple visualization technique can help you open the door and communicate with spirits. Close your eyes and take several deep breaths. Imagine you're approaching a forest. As you enter, feel the texture of the ground under your feet. Smell the evergreen trees. Hear the songs of the birds. Feel the sensation of the breeze refreshing your skin, and the air rejuvenating your energy as it enters your body. You're walking alongside a stream. The sound of the water cleanses you. A large redwood tree stands in front of you. As you approach, someone slowly steps from behind it. You recognize this person. Use your imagination to interpret the message the person has for you. This will most likely be a spirit who is attempting to communicate with you. Keep a journal of whatever comes to you that you can refer to later, but during the process, just allow it to unfold naturally without judgment.

Where Are Spirits?

I've often been asked where spirits are and if they can hear when people speak to them. The answer is that spirits are not limited to the constraints of the physical realm and actually navigate locations and dimensions with a mere thought.

During one of my workshops, a Japanese woman named Yoko welcomed a visit by her father. I had her standing in the middle of a circle while the group practiced filling up and balancing her energy. Yoko's father's spirit appeared over her right shoulder to me.

"Oh, your father's here," I said. "He's right over your right shoulder. He's very happy to be here, and he has a very bright energy."

"Where is he?" Yoko asked.

Her father began to laugh hysterically, saying that he was on the shelf at her house.

"He says he's up on a shelf, and he thinks it's hysterical."

"Yes, he's up on a shelf at my house, in a picture. I talk to him all the time."

The whole group burst out laughing.

"She thinks I'm in the graveyard in Japan," he told me with a big smile.

Yoko said, "Well, I know he's in Japan because we go to the graveyard to visit him every year in August, and he comes home with us for three days. As we walk home, we don't turn around, and we hold our hands behind us to help carry him. Once we're home, we make all the food he used to love when he was with us and celebrate his life. Then, on the third day, we bring him back to the grave. We have this ritual in Japan to honor our ancestors. Can you ask him if it's okay to have my father-in-law's picture next to him?"

"He says, 'Of course,' once again with a huge smile. Your father's soul appears to be of very high consciousness, very light."

"Yes, he was a beautiful man, a huge inspiration to all who knew him."

Yoko didn't seem surprised that her father had contacted her, although she still had a fixed idea about where he was. In some cultures, it is quite normal to continue a connection with those who have passed over, and many rituals are born of this belief. We shed the mortal coil, but the soul continues on infinitely. It was never born, and it will never die. As we align with this notion, the interconnectedness of the universe reveals itself.

A friend once told me of her experience of oneness. She was at a train station in an unfamiliar city. As she looked around the station, every single person suddenly looked and felt familiar, even though she had never seen them before.

"It was one of the most beautifully connected feelings I have ever had," she said.

Cape Town

The following story brings up an interesting question: Why focus on the spiritual dimension when we are here in this dimension? It is important to be grounded in the human experience and to be fully present and awake. But having a knowing of the spiritual dimension and integrating or remembering who and what we are can help us be more fully present in the here and now. Lingering in the human consciousness is the fear of mortality, which is derived from a finite perspective of duality and separation. By being open to experiencing a knowing of the spiritual dimension, the illusion of lack, limitation and separation disappears, and the peace and harmony of remembering that we are of the same Source—all connected, all one—becomes our natural state of homeostasis. It simply illuminates the truth, which has always been and always will be, that we are of one mind.

"She's the love of my life!"

At seventy-three years of age, Jeremy had finally reunited with his soul mate. Forty years had passed since that day in Cape Town, South Africa, when fate stepped in. She had worn an ivory chiffon summer dress, high heels, and an elegant wide-brimmed hat that almost covered her alluring gaze. Her dress, billowing with the warm breeze, escorted her into the club where Jeremy was performing. He instantly became flustered and forgot where he was in the song. He missed the chorus and had to stop playing the song altogether when the room filled with her presence. Confused and "out of his groove," he announced a short break to the audience.

When the manager found him forty-five minutes later, the couple was deeply entrenched in a blink less exchange at a small table in the rear of the club.

"What about the music? What the heck am I paying you for?" demanded the manager. Not wanting to miss a second with his new love, Jeremy grabbed her hand and stole into the night with her without a word. The warm night breeze embraced them, sealing their fate. They giggled like children, swirling in love along an enchanted lane.

They fell hard for each other and spent two weeks of soul-recognition bliss before being torn apart and thrust back into their lives with their respective spouses. It wasn't their time, but destiny reunited them four decades later.

By this time, Jeremy was well-known in the music world for his brilliance as a composer and producer. Originally from England, he now lived in Los Angeles. His tall, confident, proper English demeanor proved to be a perfect compliment to Lindsay's stunning elegance. She was sixty-eight, still drop-dead gorgeous, standing 5'7", with crystal blue-grey eyes, olive skin, and the perfect shade of silver-white hair resembling the lining of a cloud. Her hair was cut in an angled, high-fashion style, accentuating her prominent cheekbones.

Lindsay had built quite a reputation as an interior designer in South Africa, and also happened to be the World Champion speed-walker for her age group in the twenty-kilometer race. Her fit body resembled that of a thirty-year-old. Together, the chemistry of their soul connection had a logarithmic effect, greater than the sum of their individuality, which proved to be a tremendous inspiration for them both.

Jeremy brought Lindsay to me for some "hands-on healing" on her back, which had become quite burdensome of late. As we began a session together, I immediately felt Lindsay's mother's spirit come in like a sweet fragrance, awakening the senses. Her gentle, loving smile filled the room. She looked quite similar to Lindsay and emanated the same graceful energy. I sensed that Lindsay was a very open spiritual person, so I felt comfortable sharing what I felt with her.

"I feel your mother's spirit here," I said.

Lindsay's smile opened, and tears of joy poured forth as she said softly, "Oh, that's lovely. Please continue. What does she have to say?"

"She's showing me your brother, and he has doctors all around him."

"Yes, he's been ill his whole life and has developed Alzheimer's disease. He just recently had a stroke, as well," Lindsay replied.

"Your mother wants to help heal the pain this has caused you. Is that okay with you?" I asked.

"Why, yes, thank you," she agreed gracefully.

Lindsay did not reveal the details of what her mother was referring to, but I definitely felt the weight of it energetically in her body. I could feel an emotional energetic constriction around her heart. I held my left hand a few inches above her heart chakra. A river of healing energy flowed through my hand and into her body, leaving a tingling sensation in its wake through my arm and hand.

Whenever I feel this energy pass through me, it instantly puts all the mundane worries of this world in their insignificant place. I remember that this is not all that there is, that I'm not limited to this space and time. I'm a part of everything. It flows in like a cool ocean breeze, calming the sweltering heat of the mind's machinations.

"Oh, I feel a warm, open feeling in my chest," Lindsay exclaimed.

Her voice was soothing, like a warm candlelit bath. Her breath deepened as her shoulders surrendered to the table. After a few minutes, I felt her energy become completely clear.

The unwavering stillness of my mind as I concentrated on ushering in healing energy brought her energy into alignment with my stillness. When her energy became still and balanced, all of her internal resistance ceased, and I saw a deep indigo light in my mind's eye. Her deep sigh emphasized the degree of her cathartic release. I continued the communication.

"Your mother is telling me that you are extremely close to your granddaughter, and she's trying to tell me her name. She's saying a 'gab' sound."

"Yes, her name is Gabriella. I love her very much."

"Your mother is telling me that you three form a beautiful, triangular karmic connection. She wants to make sure that you stay close to your granddaughter, especially in six years when she is thirteen years old. She will have a difficult time for a while, and she will need your guidance more than ever. She will go through a period where she will feel very isolated, and you may be the only one who will be able to understand her."

"I have always felt that connection with her. Of course, I will be there for her."

Conveying prophetic messages has never been of much interest to me. I much prefer messages that can be validated in the present, but nonetheless these can be some of the more profound validations from the spiritual realm.

"She's also saying not to worry about the financial arrangement with Peter, your ex-husband. It will work out fine, so be patient and try not to worry."

"Oh, yes, I have been concerned about that," Lindsay said. "Even though I'm sure she knows this, please tell my mother that I love her, and thank you for everything."

Just as we were finishing, there was a knock on the door. Jeremy came storming in, complaining how he had just spent the last thirty-five minutes in the waiting room trying to make an international call, only to discover that his new state-of-the-art phone was unable to do it.

"Shush, darling. This is important," Lindsay abruptly stopped him.

After we finished, she explained to Jeremy what had just happened. He looked at me and said, "You're kidding me. Why, that's incredible."

He paused, looking at the floor with a rather puzzled

expression, then slowly lifted his head in conclusion. "So, Daniel, you're a medium?"

"Yes," I replied.

"Well, don't take this the wrong way, lad, but what's the point, really?"

Lindsay interjected quickly, wanting to answer for me. "By talking with my mother, he has just facilitated a tremendous amount of healing with my brother, and she also answered many questions that I've had for a very long time."

"Wow, that's something," Jeremy replied.

Lindsay's objection, although noble, proved unnecessary. I have long understood that what I do may be hard for many people to comprehend, predominantly due to the fact that it simply may not be within their belief system. And that's okay. It comes with the territory.

"Do I have any spirits around me, Daniel?" he asked a moment later.

"You have a lot of uncles around you."

"God, yes, I had five uncles, and they were all great, especially my Uncle Allister."

"Well, this can go on forever, but I must go. I have other clients waiting for me."

We all laughed. "I'll see you soon," I said.

These episodes help us remember and re-connect. They can help wake us up from the mundane and birth the passion of our soul. Often, people are so moved by the occurrence that they want to tell everyone immediately. After a person has the experience of communicating with a friend or loved one, I remind them that this is a personal gift that not everyone will understand and may possibly even ridicule. It's okay to integrate and process the feelings, but also to have discernment with whom you share these experiences.

Beyond Language

The following story addresses the question about language being a barrier and the persistence of a loving father to contact his daughter.

Annalisa had found me in her desperate search to obtain

relief from the sciatica pain she had experienced for the past five months. Her daughter, Deborah, whom I already knew, called to give me the scoop on her mother before she came to see me. Deborah felt that her mother was ready for spiritual healing and suspected that her energetic constriction was a result of burying her emotions. Deborah felt I was the perfect person to help her mother open up so she could move forward both physically and emotionally.

When I first met Annalisa, she looked as though her pain was wrapped around her like a mighty python slowly suffocating its kill. The grey veil of indifference over her dark chocolate eyes did little to hide the wounds of her betrayed love. I would later find out that she was still harboring the anger and pain that was left when her husband abandoned her and ran off with their nanny. In spite of the hardships she had endured, her genetics prevailed. She was easy on the eyes, with beautifully classic Latin features and perfect olive skin. She had aged well in her fifty-eight years. She wore her thick black hair short and fashionable. Annalisa had the posture and appearance of an upper-society lady, except a little too rigid.

When she came to see me, she had arrived at her point of surrender and admitted she needed some help. Annalisa had migrated from South America as a child to start a new life with her family in America. She had been extremely close to her father since childhood. But Annalisa's father was recently stolen from her in the middle of the night when his heart just stopped. Her marriage had already fallen apart, and the loss of her dear father was just too much for her to handle.

As we began a session together, I gently placed my hands upon her back. I felt the anger rapidly rise up like insatiable flames, almost as if the pain had found the first available outlet to make its escape. At the same time, I felt the spirit of her father enter the room. His large, proud stature allowed him to stand with confidence. His big, dark eyes, which he had given to Annalisa, were open and honest.

The kind, calm spirit of Annalisa's father was a welcome reprieve from the intensity of her cathartic emotional release. Relief swelled up and fell from her eyes, opening the floodgate to her heart. The strength of their bond was palpable. His eyes revealed the unconditional love only a parent could give. She was safe in his presence.

His name was Juan. He had grown up in Mexico City before the revolution, before his parents disappeared in the bloodshed of the war. Annalisa's mother had been a hard woman. Her mother had abandoned her at an early age, leaving her and her two brothers to be raised by her father. He did the best that he could with limited finances and working as a ranch hand in Mexico.

Annalisa and her father naturally gravitated toward one another, as they were of the same character and temperament. This was obvious, and it had alienated them further from her mother. Still, I could feel that the gentle, kind demeanor of her father was all about unconditional love.

His spirit approached me with sincere purity of heart, wanting me to relay a message to Annalisa. I explained that I felt the spirit of her father in the room. Her large brown eyes beckoned for the chance to connect with her father again.

"That's beautiful, but can I talk to him?"

"Yes, I can convey what he has to say if you are open to that."

Detained only by the dogma of her religious upbringing, she tentatively agreed. "Yes, yes, that would be so nice," she said.

I began to relay the information from her father. "Annalisa, I'm sorry that your mother wasn't there for you. I know it caused you tremendous heartache. I want to help free you of the despair."

This validation from the spirit world evoked a shudder through her body.

"Yes, I would like that. I love my father."

I witnessed the infusion of love he gave her from the spiritual realm. The deep indigo light energy filled her. It was like he poured his love into her energetically. A whoosh of tense energy left her, and her body fell limp as she let out a sigh. A peace beyond human understanding pervaded the room.

"I am with you and still protecting you, my mariposa," he said.

With this, Annalisa burst out crying once again, knowing without a doubt that this was the spirit of her father. Mariposa had been his special nickname for her.

"He only spoke Spanish. How could you understand him?" Annalisa asked.

I had experienced this before and explained to her that communication with spirits supersedes the limitations of our tangible finite reality and language, a realm where direct communication is possible telepathically. I slowly opened my eyes as the spirit of her father faded, still smiling from within and bathing in the beauty of the transcendent energy in the room. Annalisa's eyes met mine with the vulnerability and gratitude that come with the baring of one's soul and the gift of truly being seen.

My Sweet Beloved

An angelic voice beckons my heart to burst with laughter
Restraints from form gone hereafter
The illustrious light of these smiling eyes softens the breath
Heartfelt kindness pours through, soothing my soul
I remember now
There you are, my sweet beloved

—Daniel Ryan

Chapter 18

Transdimensional Healing

It always seems impossible until it is done.

—*Nelson Mandela*

A physical medium has the capacity to facilitate the transference of healing energy from the spiritual realm. This healing energy, not limited by the physical laws of nature in the earthly realm, is transformational. It is infinite in nature, and can and does allow miracles to happen. But you must remember that miracles are only considered miracles because they don't fit into existing belief systems. They are unexplainable by the physical laws of nature in this dimension.

During spirit communication, I have witnessed this phenomenon often. The transcendent healing energy is evoked in different ways and is not limited to a specific "qualified healer or medium." It is based on the faith of the healer in trusting that perfect healing is taking place, regardless of the appearance. The greater the detachment to the results of the healing, the more powerful and complete it will be. The energy has the power to reverse disease and dysfunction in our physical, mental, emotional, and spiritual bodies. It has the power to alter an undesired genetic expression that can prevent or reverse the disease process.

To facilitate the transference of this transcendental cosmic vibration, you must become a clear channel by releasing all negative energetic patterns within yourself (see the next chapter, "Healing the Healer") and release all attachments to the results. This is done by utilizing the infinite capacity of the right brain to allow the transformational energy to enter hindrance-free. In other words, check your logical brain at the door. The door to the infinite realm and the key to that door is your imagination. If you were only to rely on what you currently know or what you believe is real, you would certainly become stuck. Through the following simple steps, you can enter into the realm of infinite possibilities and experience the power of manifestation within.

BREATHE: Being present in the body can be a portal to the divine. By focusing your attention on breathing, you will be in the present moment. Breathing is happening in real time. If you are not in the moment, you will limit your capacity to tap into the infinite realm. If you focus on the past, your attention is on what has already happened, and this will take you out of the present moment. If you focus on the future, it will create anxiety because you are attempting to make decisions based on speculation when you don't have all the information yet.

As you exhale, allow your breath to release anything that isn't revealing the greatest expression of your soul. Release all the ideas of what you think you need to get or do, and allow your soul to speak through you. Your identities as a father, mother, student, contractor, dentist, yoga instructor, etc., are all ideas of who you think you are. They are only a fraction of your unexpressed greater potential. This cathartic release is tending to your garden to expedite the seeds of your soul to grow in fertile soil. Your intuition or "gut feeling" will tell you what is holding you back as you listen in real time.

IMAGINE: The door to all creativity is in the right side or the non-linear, non-logical aspect of the brain. Imagination lives here and will be your vehicle to transport you beyond your perceived limitations. By quieting the left-brain or linear, logical brain, you can hear the one voice of Universal Intelligence. It will simply percolate to the surface very naturally. Notice that aspect of you that is observing all the ideas that your mind creates. This is the One Mind or Universal Intelligence that is observing the small self. Shifting your attention to the One Mind, you automatically have an all-access pass to the universe.

PRAYER AND MEDITATION: Again, the power of prayer and meditation has been proven to be very effective in utilizing these principles. By being passionate while praying, you are creating a feeling tone of that which you are focused on and accessing the power of manifestation. By visioning and setting an intention based on your intuition, meditation will provide you with divine inspiration.

VISIONING: Visioning happens very naturally as we surrender identities, attachments, and expectations. Visioning is catching your soul's greatest desire for expression and acting upon it. Doors will open, and there will be a quickening at an exponential pace as you come into alignment with the soul's yearning. Being passionate, resolute, and maintaining the feeling tone of your soul's vision will bring it into manifestation by our natural capacity to create. The more passionate you are about holding a vision, the quicker and more complete it will be. Competitiveness and comparison will fall away and become unnecessary. Ultimately, this will abolish all barriers and lead to the realization of oneness of all people, places, and things.

Transdimensional Energy Transference

This energy is a high-vibration light frequency that increases the speed of vibration of that with which it comes into contact. The higher the vibration something becomes, the less it is limited to the physical laws of nature. It's as if you took the lid off a container, and that container is the logical mind.

As you've seen in many of the stories in this book, the energy is usually a deep purple or indigo color as it is transferred into the physical realm. It is not limited by physical boundaries and can permeate all levels of the tangible realm. It usually comes in as a funnel or cylinder shape, and pours directly into the person it is intended for.

I have frequently seen the light energy separate into five

horizontal grids about one to two inches apart in an anterior to posterior anatomical plane—the anterior being the abdomen and the posterior being the back. Once settled into the body, electric connections develop between the planes of energy, much the same way that neurological synapses function physiologically in the body or an electrical arch does in a circuit.

This transcendental cosmic healing energy permeates the very helix of the DNA or the chain of genes waiting to be triggered and expressed. As this occurs, I believe it can alter the genetic expression of the DNA or inhibit or change how disease develops or progresses. We can also produce this energy to a degree on the physical plane by positive visioning, as described earlier. The difference is that the healing energy transferred from the spiritual realm or fourth dimension is pure and has a high halcyon vibration that is not subject to the limited beliefs and energetic patterns of the earthly realm or the predominate third dimensional reality. This energy eliminates the stuck energy patterns by illuminating them, much the same as exposing a shadow to light. This allows the innate intelligence within all beings to function optimally. Within the third dimensional human reality exists a hardwired fight or flight mechanism that was necessary for the evolution of the human consciousness. As we evolve and integrate and allow more and more of the fourth dimension, our attention is directed towards the utilization of the power of creation through accessing our innate potential. Quite simply, it's being the creative source to express your souls greatest desires as opposed to the third dimensional reality of trying to get or make something happen. You are the source!

Chapter 19

Healing the Healer

All you need is love.

—*The Beatles*

There are many challenges for the healer to contemplate through introspection as he or she engages in the opportunity to heal others. However, there are really only two choices: love or fear. It is always an honor to help others with their healing processes. Entering into the sacred space where you can help others heal is a responsibility, and it is most beneficial if taken seriously with altruistic intentions. Your innate capacity to heal already exists, but the work is in removing the barriers that prevent it from expressing fully through you.

The Door Opens Inward

There are so many external distractions in this world that it's been the challenge of the ages to simply be still and turn your attention inward. My experience in working with thousands of people over the years has shown that the majority of people live in their heads, so it's no wonder their bodies hurt! If you ignore the body, it will let you know one way or another, be it through disease or dysfunction. Being present in the body can be a portal to the divine. As we turn our attention inward, the body functions as a very precise barometer and becomes a great revealer. Our awareness illuminates stagnant energetic patterns that are present in our being and transmutes them, allowing our body, mind, and spirit to function optimally.

There is a simple method that is very effective in disengaging the mind. As I said before, this exercise is simple, but it may not always be easy. As you breathe deeply, follow your breath down into your lungs and just feel the physical sensation of the air expanding your abdomen and chest cavity. Breathe deeply into the abdomen. Notice all of the different physical sensations and pay close attention to them. The most important aspect of this very simple exercise is just to notice what you are physically feeling without judgment, without analyzing it. The moment you analyze it, you are back in your head, and nothing gets healed in this vast sea of projection and sociological conditioning. The mind is a wonderful tool to be used appropriately, but ultimately it is balance that provides a solid foundation for healing from the heart out.

As you turn your attention deep into the body, you will feel sensations, usually physical at first. Eventually, you will feel the underlying emotion locked in your body physiologically via cellular memories. As you begin to feel these different sensations, they may only be fleeting at first because you'll start to analyze them. This means your attention has become mental again. When this occurs, begin again, back to focusing on the breath, and following it down into the body. Simply notice any and all sensations from the perspective of an observer.

At first, you may find that you are only able to stay present in the body for a few seconds before you're back into your head. Be patient, be still, allow the mind to relax, and try again. There is genius in simplicity, which can be observed within the stillness. The beauty of this process is the notion that there is nothing to be fixed. Still observation will illuminate your stagnant energies. The clarity of still observation provides a very powerful catalyst for the transmutation of these stagnant energies bound within your being. You will find that this illumination simply reveals the perfection that already exists within you.

Releasing Cellular Memories

Pain is directly proportional to your resistance to feeling the pain, be it conscious or unconscious. Consequently, through the power of quiet non-judgmental observation, anything that is not the truth of your being simply falls away, restoring the perception of wholeness and perfection that has always been present. I like the analogy of doors, in which some are opening and some are closing. By conscious choice, why would you attempt to keep a closing door open? (I'll leave that one to the psychologists.)

Surrender and acceptance of what is will allow you to shift your attention and energy to what's unfolding right before your eyes. From this place, we are pulled very naturally into the vortex of the divine alchemy, revealing itself gracefully in spite of the ego's agenda. As you focus your attention on your physical sensations, it's very likely these sensations will reveal a deeper level of energetic stagnation. As layers of an onion are peeled away, the body releases these energetic patterns as a way of illuminating outdated belief systems.

Therein lies the beauty . . . your beauty. Just being is enough. There is nowhere to get to and nothing to do except being as a state of mind. As deep-seated, dormant cellular memories are released by the power of your attention, you may experience them in varying degrees as they dissolve in your body. I have oftentimes suggested to people that they receive professional psychological support during this time if they would like to discover a deeper understanding of the memories' origins. In addition to illuminating the cellular memories through your presence, removing structural imbalances in the body can also unlock and release energy to enhance healing. Disease and dysfunction occur as a result of the imbalance between the physical, emotional, and spiritual bodies. Cellular memories can be attributed to the experiences one has throughout life on these different levels. The body, mind, and spirit have an intelligence of their own that people may not be aware of on a conscious level. This is important because we have to understand how all of these different forces can counteract and destabilize one another. How can one element of your being have a clear vision and direction if you have a conflicting belief system negating its progress? These imbalances require a tremendous amount of energy to live with day to day. The wasted energy could otherwise be used for much more productive purposes.

When the cellular memories are eradicated, your body can achieve homeostasis, which frees up all that energy to allow you to fulfill a truer expression of your soul's intention. As these cellular memories are released, you may re-experience them on some level as they are leaving your being. This can cause a concern for some people, but it normally resolves within a couple of days. The important thing to do at this point is nothing. Just observing what is happening with the power of your awareness is enough to assist the stagnant energy in moving through and out of your being. It is common for people to feel lighter and more peaceful after this natural expansion of consciousness occurs.

Beyond Survival

The evolution of the soul through many incarnations has developed an incredible fight or flight mechanism that needs to be recognized and integrated before it is transcended. This mechanism has been essential in the evolutionary process and now needs to be transcended to allow the paradigm shift to the fourth dimension that is currently taking place in human consciousness. However this cannot be done with the limited perspective of the finite mind because it cannot be transcended and integrated from within the survival mechanism.

Recognizing the Matrix

First one must recognize that you are within the mechanism matrix. It has become such an integral part of our being that we are completely identified with it and don't even question it's necessity. We are it! Whenever one's energy feels "stuck" you can be sure that the survival mechanism is fully engaged. If you are judging yourself or others, if you feel you are a victim, or you are looking for something to save you outside of yourself you are "in it" and it cannot be resolved from within it, the finite mind.

We are often times our own harshest judge. When will you arrive, feel complete, feel content, know that you have accomplished enough? From within the matrix the answer is never. Yes you will have temporary reprieves from the critical nature of the judge but it won't last.

Do you ever feel like it is happening to you? That someone or something is controlling your destiny and you are simply powerless over the situation? The victim is an integral part of the matrix as well.

Who will save your soul? Is it someone or something external? This belief perpetuates a limited idea that you are not enough and creates a sense of separation and isolation from within the matrix of the survival mechanism. The truth is that we are all emanations of the one source and are necessary specific parts of the same amazing puzzle. None of which can be comprehended from within the matrix or the confines of the finite mind.

Allowing the Shift

I specifically use the idea of allowing because in order to allow the expansion of consciousness into the fourth dimension one must unlearn acting upon the unrelenting nature of the hyper vigilant survival mechanism. In other words first one must recognize that one is within the matrix and secondly resist attempting to change, fix or do anything about it other than allow it to be as it is. It is an integral part of our evolutionary process and the fact that it is so strong is something to be grateful for as opposed to the idea that it is something that needs to be eradicated from our existence. It has helped us survive and it's not going anywhere! The problem is that being completely identified with it causes an uncontrollable and reactive state of existence.

Recognizing the nature of the mechanism from within it, and consciously choosing not to try to fix or change it etc. is paramount. Simply by placing your attention on it, recognizing it and doing nothing else, allows space for the forth dimension to be integrated. This transmutation happens by surrendering the control of the survival mechanism or our limited nature and allows our infinite nature to come to the forefront. We simply become more our selves, we are not getting anything externally. As our infinite nature is integrated we understand the we are responsible for all that we create for better and for worse and our reality becomes a conscious choice from a place of empowerment. Halleluiah!

Unlocking Your Infinite Healing Potential

It is only in the process of surrender and letting go of what we think we know that we can allow infinite healing to occur.

Infinite healing, being undefined and limitless, is not limited to existing information or belief systems. Understanding this principle is crucial to allowing the power of the universe to work through you and letting your imagination lead you to a new knowing. This has been proven through enhanced performance in athletes by exclusively doing visualization exercises. Things may not always make sense from the perspective of the logical mind, but you will experience a knowing that you must trust. This knowing will surpass human understanding and, when yielded to, will produce phenomenal results. Letting go can be the difficult part. This is why practice is imperative.

With practice, you may find an interesting shift in your perspective in all areas of your life. The interconnectedness of all things suddenly becomes more obvious as you stop, look, and listen. Notice the rhythm of the breath. Feel the sensation of the breath expanding and contracting the lungs. Feel all the physical sensations occurring just as they are. There is no need to decipher and derive any profound meaning from it.

The profundity is simple and beyond the dialogue of the mind. There is no need to try to fully understand the nature of the illusion of duality because the truth of non-duality will reveal itself in the stillness. Always look for the love, and love will always reveal itself. If you don't like what you see, there may be an attachment to what it looks like. The gift is always there, but your vision of it may be askew if it cannot be seen yet. Practice patience. Practice peace and non-violence to yourself and others. This alone will change the way you see the world.

Fall for freedom as your soul's intention carries you effortlessly. Pioneer a new way of seeing, being, and loving. Seeing and being seen is the basis for all healing. The silence is deafening, and the symphony of the eternal is always playing. The beauty unfolds brilliantly as the habitual monotony is shattered. Do something differently! Challenge yourself to a new perspective on an old situation. What have you got to lose except that which you don't need? You have your whole life to gain. Have you stopped and contemplated what the hurry is all about? Where your mind is going? Have you ever contemplated who's observing your mind's chatter?

The Perception of Perfection

There is an aspect of you that has never been harmed, betrayed, or abused in any way, shape or form. You are whole, perfect and complete as you are. This concept may seem abstract while you are submerged in the human experience, but see if you can allow yourself for a moment to contemplate the following. As we navigate through the human physical realm, we are provided opportunities for a greater realization and expression of our soul's desires. From the human finite perspective, things happen to us that render us dysfunctional, such as being born into a dysfunctional family, being abused, illness, loss of wealth, etc.

Before we were born into physical form, we made an agreement to be presented with different trials and tribulations for the advancement of our soul. Our soul was never born and will never die. Consequently, what appear to be bad things happening to us is actually an opportunity for our souls to evolve. The infinite perspective is completely opposite from the limited human perspective.

It is just like a seed pod in the forest that may lie dormant for many years until awakened by a fire to create new growth. That seed pod isn't harmed by the fire, but actually needs the fire to initiate an awakening of its potential to become a new tree. In the same way, greater consciousness is always being birthed in conjunction with the infinite capacity of the universe expressing itself, constantly seeking more ways to participate in this incredible co-creative process of God experiencing itself as you. From the perspective of perfection and wholeness, it's really all about revealing the untapped potential that already exists within you. You don't need to work for it or create it. It only needs to be realized. This can be done by shifting your attention to a perspective of "perfection."

Stop, look, and listen before you allow your mind to catapult you into the idea that something is "good" or "bad." Things "just are," and they are perfect as they are. By experimenting with this concept, you will begin questioning and challenging existing belief systems that are playing on autopilot, and wake you up front and center into the now.

You may be surprised at how those things that you previously categorized as "bad" or "good" actually "feel" as you see and feel them for the first time. When you de-compartmentalize an idea or belief and allow yourself to realize what "is"— just as it is—you can begin again. You have an opportunity to be fully engaged in the co-creative process of the universe. This ignites the love, joy, passion, and peace that are your birthright.

Home

The waterfall of love flows freely from our hearts as one
A decree for all to see our time has come
This divine alchemy shall surely change the world from
*   inside-out for it*
Paves the way for us all to remember
Blessed be those who surrender only to find the pearly gates
*   behind them*
Time to smile, time to be still, time to celebrate
The magical essence of love fills the air with all the excite-
*   ment of a new beginning*
Infused by our passion for one another
We fall freely into the arms of our eternal beloved
Knowing we are home

—Daniel Ryan

Chapter 20

The Sacred Circle

Geometry existed before the creation.

—*Plato*

When Pythagoras shared his vision of geometry with the world, he knew a secret. Just like in the parables of Christ, many sacred mysteries in geometry reveal the higher exaltation of the soul. Sacred geometry has been utilized throughout the ages in the form of gem and crystal formation, architecture, and human ritual, to name a few. While integrating cosmic transdimensional healing in workshops, I teach and utilize sacred geometry to magnify the power of the energy being transferred from the spiritual realm.

The most powerful geometric configuration of all is the circle. The circle represents oneness, where there is no beginning and no end. In the circle, the veil of separation is lifted as individual expressions of Universal Intelligence, or God, are united in the tangible realm. In other words, it is a vibration that enables people to wake up and remember who they are as perfect emanations of God or the one Source.

You are not only your physical appearance, job, or whatever you are identified with in society. You are a perfect expression of the God Source or Universal Intelligence waiting to become more of itself. In the sacred circle, those soul qualities yearning to be expressed through you are given a voice that must be heard! It is each individual's mandate to contribute his or her specific calling to the world. Within the sacred circle, in recognition of oneness, a quickening happens that elevates the energy vibration for all.

My First Group Meeting

Guided by intuition and divine intervention, I know that one of my main roles here in this dimension is to teach and assist healers in their healing, in order to magnify the effect for all. In meditation, I felt called to expand my reach in the world. I knew I had to begin working with larger audiences to empower others. I kept feeling that April 20th was the date to hold the first gathering. I checked the calendar, and it was open. I booked a space, and the universe took over. Everything fell into place effortlessly. The tide of the universal mind had risen above the limitations of my finite mind, drowning out the noise of fear, lack and limitation. I had the awareness of something much bigger at work, and I was grateful to be conscious enough to surrender to it.

I had a vision of working on a much larger scale. Seeing one person at a time began to feel limited. Without knowing how it would unfold, I allowed Spirit to move me beyond that which I knew. I had the courage to show up and trust that the spirits would appear, and that transcendental healing would take place, especially since *they* had scheduled it. I was as curious as the next guy about what was going to happen. I had no control, and in this act of surrender, the slate was clean for anything to happen, and it did.

One day, our year-and-a-half-old daughter looked at a painting over our bed and said, "Angels singing." I said to my wife, "Now we know what it looks like when angels sing." As I heard this I felt a door open within, the small identification I had of myself became clear and I felt borderless and expansive. As they say, the teacher appears when the student is ready. I felt one step closer to my life's purpose.

More than double the number of people expected showed

up at my first gathering. I organized the chairs in a circle and placed a vase of roses from my garden in the center. Then I placed three candles around them. My friend, Jai, played Tibetan bowls before the meditation and his wife, Savanna, sang like an angel from heaven. Incense that I had brought back from India was burning. It was a full-on California gathering. As the people arrived, the circle's energy was elevated to a heightened state. As one person received a transmission and healing, the whole group shifted and expanded with that person. With each revealing, the veil between the physical and spiritual realm became more transparent.

The physical boundaries that normally exist disappeared. We were one. This was the unraveling of the belief of separation for all who attended. I felt that I had fully stepped into my power and had accepted my calling. It was as if I had just taken a step, and it all became clear. All the machinations of the mind became a whisper. My intuition, which used to be a whisper, became a very conscious, distinct voice that felt natural and easy as it moved through me. Actually, the "me" wasn't as significant any longer.

Jai, the Tibetan bowl master, performed during the meditation. It was nothing short of magical, with the tones from these ancient bowls reverberating through every cell of each person in the room. A non-verbal transmission happened, as the door to another dimension opened. The message that Jai received during the healing circle came from his mother. She told him not to worry, that she would always be with him and she loved him dearly. This spurred a discussion during the question-and-answer phase near the close of the gathering.

One question was: "If a message comes through, does that mean that a person has passed?" Jai's mother was still living. The higher self can communicate a message even if the person is still living and, in fact, I often feel another living person's energy around someone when they're thinking of them or praying for them.

Savanna, Jai's wife, called me a week later. She explained that Jai had two mothers—a birth mother and an adoptive mother. She asked me if I knew which mother I was referring to when I gave him the message in the circle. Actually, I didn't recall what I had said to Jai that night. I assured her that one thing I knew for sure is that the message is always perfect, even if it does not appear to be so at the time. But she insisted on knowing which mother I thought it was, promising to explain after assuring me there was a specific reason for this question.

I explained that I wasn't "online" at the moment, but I again reassured her that the message is always perfect and will often make sense later, even if not at the present.

Savanna became very quiet and continued in a whisper, "The reason I was asking is that Jai's adoptive mother passed away unexpectedly that Friday, only four days after the sacred circle."

I reassured her that it must have been his adoptive mother that was sending him one last message from her higher self before she shed the mortal coil. On some level, she knew that her passing was imminent and was putting her affairs in order. This also made sense regarding the date that kept coming to me in meditation in the days preceding the group meeting. I kept hearing that I was supposed to do the meeting on Monday, April 20th. I assumed that this message was Spirit nudging me along to get out there and begin doing larger gatherings, but there were several reasons that this date was significant. This was only one. I knew that this experience was challenging Savanna's current belief systems about life and death, hence the inquiry.

Once people get a taste of the spiritual realm, it changes them forever. A door is opened that expands their interest in re-connecting with Source. It initially causes confusion when the logical mind attempts to make sense of the spiritual realm. Of course, this doesn't work because this logic is based in the finite realm, where all things are limited. Communication with the spiritual realm is infinite, where all things are possible. When first experienced, it may take some time to integrate this knowing and expansion of consciousness.

As I moved forward in faith, I received an immediate response from the universe. Spirit was having its way with me, through me. As a result, my next gathering doubled in attendance. The room was electrifying, saturated in love. I was fully aware that a greater power was at work. I was grateful to be a witness to Spirit working through me.

My First House Meeting

My first in-house gathering was at a friend's house. We had just returned from a trip to Hawaii, and my internal clock was still off. I wasn't feeling very connected and clear because I had decreased my meditation and increased my desserts!

I arrived early to meditate in a separate room of the house before the event started. After everyone arrived (fifteen in all, including one pregnant woman who counted for two), I entered the room and sat down. After a brief introduction, I led a guided meditation.

After the twenty-minute mediation ended, we all gazed at one another in the circle. I realized that I didn't feel or see any spirits around!

"This is my worst nightmare," I thought. It was what I had feared most about going public. Well, I thought, I should do something. So I stood up and intuitively approached people to tune into them to do energy readings. I was nervous because of self-imposed expectations, but I was determined to overcome them.

I began to read a woman to my right, who turned out to be deeply identified with her co-dependent patterns, but had a nice heart chakra opening in spite of it. I began to relax more by the second person I read to my left. I noticed a spirit, someone's brother, in my peripheral vision to my right, where two middle-aged women sat. I asked if anyone over there had a brother who had passed. Only silence and blank stares were returned with my question.

My attention turned to Laura, the pregnant woman. Her baby had a message for her. She requested the father to be home more often. The father, a surgeon, worked long hours. She also wanted her mother to be more positive and confident because she felt and absorbed everything. The baby also gave Laura advice on how to help her parents connect better.

My attention then went to the two ladies across the circle. Their fathers wanted to communicate. They said they both had fathers on the other side. Then the brother showed up again, and one of the ladies admitted that she did have a brother on the other side, but she hadn't wanted to draw attention to herself before.

"Help a guy out, will you?" I joked.

Just then, another spirit drew my attention to the left. He said he was Laura's grandfather and said the name "Trinity." Then Laura, the pregnant woman, said that was the name of the retirement community where her grandmother lived. I learned that the spirits can be connected to anyone in the room, not necessarily the person I'm talking to or have my hands on. He then told me the name "Rye." Laura said that "Rye" is her maiden name.

And so it went for two hours that disappeared into what seemed like twenty minutes. A total of nine spirits came through that afternoon. I was out of time and space and completely relaxed and quite relieved that it had been a very successful afternoon. It was a perfect day to help me embody trust on a deeper level. Even when we don't feel connected to Source, we are. As the sun rises and reflects across the ocean, the light appears to be broken between the waves, but it's not. The light of the sun is only separated by the reflection in the waves, but the beam itself is never broken.

The Council

As I facilitate sacred circles, a council in the spiritual realm guides me. Participants are placed together based on similar resonating energetic tones or stagnant patterns that need illumination. I say "illumination" because it's not that there is something wrong, but I see these patterns as untapped potential.

As I continued to hold gatherings, they proved to be an instant success. The next one filled up within four hours and was beyond capacity before I could send out an e-mail to inform people that it was full. We all got cozy, and I knew that everyone in attendance was there for a reason if only two or two thousand it didn't matter.

My prayer was "use me," and the spirits did. For the first time, I became aware of a council in the spiritual realm that was giving me instructions on what to do with the group. Completely immersed in the moment with my logical mind aside, I followed directions. They instructed me about whom they wanted to stand up and be placed into the center of the circle.

As I place people in circles together, I am not usually told why they are together until later, as the purpose unfolds in the moment.

During one gathering, I called up a man and a woman who didn't know each other. The man was to facilitate her healing while the group around them sent healing energy to them. They stood face-to-face, and he held his hands up toward her. She began to shed layer after layer of energy. As the layers fell away, tears fell from her eyes. She clasped his right wrist and put his hand on her upper chest and held it there. Not a word was spoken for several minutes as we all participated in this dramatic revealing. After the meeting, the woman who had been in the center of the circle told me she had never experienced such a deep healing, and her heart now felt pure. She hugged me in deep gratitude.

Three women were up next, and the council told me they all had a common fear of moving forward. One of the women served as a ground for the other two. A funnel of energy from above formed and then connected these women. Many of the healers in attendance could see the energy. Others only felt it. This was very powerful to witness.

Two more women were chosen to stand up. They didn't know one another but were sitting together. The spirits told me they were mother and daughter in a past life. They shed tears of joy and recognition as they looked into one another. They both told me later that, before we started, they loved each other the instant they saw one another. That was why they had sat together. One said that earlier she had placed her head on the other's shoulder, as a child would do to her mother.

The next group of women, six in all, came up. One woman's mother's spirit said the word "Japanese." The woman covered her mouth and, with a gasp, bent forward slightly. After composing herself, she told us their family used to call her "mama-san," even though she wasn't Japanese. Then I could see that all of the six women standing had their mothers in the spiritual realm, standing next to their daughters. The council told me that one of the women had lost her five-year-old son to leukemia, and they wanted her to know that all of the mothers on the other side were watching over her little Jacob. A wave of energy instantly exploded and reverberated out through everyone, as if a strong wind had pushed everyone off balance backward. There wasn't a dry eye in the house.

At a previous circle, Jacob, the five-year-old boy, came through to speak to his grandmother who was in attendance. He was trying to tell me something. It sounded like "moh, moh," but I didn't think I was hearing it right. When I repeated this to his grandmother, she instantly covered her mouth with a gasp and burst out crying. After she caught her breath, she explained that Jacob was always trying to say "more, more," but that's how he pronounced it. He wanted to play more. Everyone was stunned into a silent awe. She said that he passed away in her arms in the hospital, and that was the last thing he said to her: He wanted to play more.

So it continued until everyone in attendance had been up in a circle within a circle to join in the healing. Next, the group had me stand, and they sent me energy, for which I was grateful. A few of the seers in the group gave me a message from all the spirits in attendance. They said thank you, and that they appreciated what I was doing.

The Last Dance

During a Sacred Circle Eric said that he felt connected to a woman in the circle.

Her name was Judy I had them both stand up. As they stood facing each other their connection percolated to the surface like memories encased in bubbles, as if it had been buried deep at sea for many years. As they starred into one another's eyes Eric spoke;

"I feel as though I want to hold your hand above your head and spin you around, it almost like I know you from another lifetime."

The energy in the room became more dense and swirled all around and through everyone.

"I'm seeing water, it's dark, very dark," Judy said.

As I observed it came to me how they were connected, I saw that Eric had been Judy's daughter in a past life. Prior to this past life inquires didn't hold much interest for me as I thought that it was difficult to validate, but this felt different.

"The left side of your head looks dark for some reason," Eric said.

"There is something floating in the water next to me and I feel like I'm sinking," Judy said.

"I see that you had a cut across your forehead above your left eye and temple," I said.

With each remembrance I felt a wave of energy expand out to all in attendance validating every epiphany.

"I'm getting the year 1912," Eric said.

"My name is eve and you are my father," Eric said.

The room continued to become more and more transcendent energetically.

"The Titanic!!!" Eric and I blurted out at exactly the same time. Two others in the circle also said it at the same time.

A tsunami of energy exploded in the diameter around them as if another dimension had blown wide open. I witnessed everyone in the circle repel back as the wave pushed through them. This experience left everyone in the room absolutely sure that this in fact was true by the energetic validation conveyed. To my surprise this experience was greater validation than anything from our tangible realm and lent itself to a new perspective on the burden of proof. After researching the facts later in the evening I discovered that they were all in fact accurate.

The Train

At the sacred circles I encourage attendees to participate in using the group to practice honing their intuitive healing skills. Kelly was feeling her grandmother around and I had her stand up in the center of the circle to get a feel for this experience in front of a group, which is quite different than one on one. She saw her grandmother Amah in a wheelchair. Aaron was feeling connected to her grandmother as well and I had him stand up and face her.

Amah began showing Aaron a swinging motion with one arm and then Aaron suddenly felt a pulling motion from behind him and asked Robert to come up. Robert was seeing his own grandfather slamming his fist down on a table. Kelly recognized this as similar signs of the anger and abuse in her own family, her grandmother would swing a switch to discipline her children. The table was significant to Kelly as she remembered often times the parents fists would come down onto it with a fury in anger and frustration. The pieces of the puzzle were coming together. I was quietly walking around them as they were processing the experience.

As I walked by Holly, a woman that I had conveyed a heartfelt message from her father a few minutes earlier, her fathers spirit stopped me and showed me a picture of a train. I asked Holly if that meant anything to her. Her head fell forward with a sigh and it took a minute for her to respond. I felt that this was intensely personal to the core and I assured her that it was okay to keep it to her self if she wished.

Holly slowly lifted her head and spoke softly through her fogged glasses and tears. "I do know what he means by the train, you see his father, my grandfather, was abused on a train when he was just a boy and that's when the cycle of abuse began." Holly's last name was also Kelly.

This scenario was not unique, the theme and synchronicity of these intermingled stories was not coincidental as it is yet another example of how it is organized by the spiritual realm. Our job is to trust and allow it to unfold as it is.

Jesus once said, "These things and greater you shall also do." People are oftentimes too willing to project their power or accept it for others, but not themselves. I have gone into great detail in describing my process of unfolding in part to dispel the illusion that I can do something that others are not capable of. Projection (or denial) of one's magnificence does not benefit the healer or the person receiving the healing for greater empowerment.

When someone says, "I can't do what you do," or "I don't see what you see." I say, "Thank God!" Wouldn't life be boring if we were all contributing the same thing? We are here to get out of the way of ourselves and align with our soul's *unique* yearning for expression. Once we find out what makes our soul sing, our mandate is to express those gifts in any way shape or form possible, this is true happiness.

Chapter 21

Now Is the Beginning

Knowing is not enough; we must apply.
Willing is not enough; we must do.

—*Johann Wolfgang von Goethe*

The spiritual path is not for the weak. We choose each moment. It takes a tremendous amount of courage at times to hold fast in the present moment, all while navigating through the maze of challenges and illusions presented as we step into our greater potential as spiritual beings having a human experience. The following insights are intended to provide assistance as you embark upon your personal journey.

Raising Your Vibration

Now is the beginning. Step into your divinity and liberate your soul! By raising your vibration, you can attune to higher realms of consciousness. This will lift you out of density and the limited perception of the physical and astral plane. Having your consciousness lodged in these lower planes limits your ability to understand the expansiveness of your own divinity.

Again, meditation is one of the fastest ways to raise your vibration. Also, ask the question, "What feeds my soul?" By asking the question, you can be present in the moment and choose consciously. This gives you an opportunity to choose differently from the repetitive unconscious "mind loop" thought patterns that will decide for you if you're not paying attention. The actions you take and the decisions you make can catapult you into a greater awareness.

During my career, I have had the opportunity to participate in many great adventures. One of my clients with whom I developed a close relationship happened to be a famous singer at the peak of her international fame. Our relationship presented me with a tremendous epiphany.

Over time, I became nervous when I was about to interact with her, although I wasn't sure why. When I turned inward to examine where this feeling was originating from, I discovered that I had fallen in love with her. It didn't feel like romantic love; it just felt pure and unconditional, which was also confusing for me at the time.

I came to the conclusion that I needed to release the energy from my body by telling her how I felt. The next time I saw her, I told her that I needed to speak with her. I looked her in the eye and told her that I had discovered I loved her.

She asked, "What is that supposed to mean?"

I answered, "I don't know, but I just needed to tell you how I felt."

Immediately, my body was freed from the shackles of one of my belief systems about love. I felt light again—and a bit silly because I wasn't sure what had happened. By identifying and expressing the emotion, bound-up energy was released, and I felt free and light again. The belief system that I held unconsciously had been clogging my energy field. It occurred to me that I had expanded my awareness about love. Love is unconditional and boundless, and cannot be limited by the finite mind.

We never spoke of this moment again, but our friendship and professional relationship continued with a new understanding between us. When our eyes met, the mutual soul recognition resonated with non-duality, or oneness, that reverberated unconditional love of another human being. It was the transcendental effect of seeing, and being seen.

Attachment

One definition of attachment is holding onto a fixed idea of how something is supposed to be. This ultimately catapults you into the past as your mind attempts to categorize and relate to it from a previous experience. This will only create disappointment because your new experiences will not be the same as the first, even if it's a better experience. For example, if you expect it to snow on Christmas and it doesn't, you may not be able to enjoy the holiday if you can't accept the way it actually is. Also, having a rigid idea of what the future will bring causes stress because you don't have enough information to envision the future yet, simply because you are not there. Having said that, it's a wonderful idea to set an intention and envision what you wish to manifest. Be open to what it looks like. It's pretty much guaranteed it won't look like you expect it to much of the time.

Manifesting

As you create a vision, it's vital to hold a feeling tone of that which you choose to create. If you choose excellent health, then visualize and imagine a feeling tone in your body of vibrant health pulsating through your veins. If it's financial freedom you choose, create a feeling tone in your body of what that would be like for you.

If you can hold the tone without canceling it out with negativity, it will come into manifestation. This is where it gets tricky because there is an incessant flow of lack and limitation in our consciousness. We are all subject to it if we don't do what it takes through meditation to bring it to the conscious mind so we have the ability to choose differently from a place of awareness.

As your intuition leads you down the path of your soul's greatest expression, your direction will change as it unfolds, so your job is to look for the open door and step through it. Your perception is a work in progress, constantly evolving, so be aware of the endless possibilities coming your way and consider utilizing them.

Through the Eyes of a Child

With the weight of the transgressions of the world on our minds, it's a miracle anything gets accomplished at all. As the mind slows down, you can create gaps in time that will reveal to you the present moment. You can see the miracle that is unfolding right in front of you. Noticing where your attention is will help you have dominion over your consciousness and empower you to make decisions from a place of high resolve.

Everyone has experienced this "no time phenomenon" that occurs when the mind is still. It usually happens during an extenuating circumstance when one is catapulted from the monotonous existence of daily repetition: when a death or a car accident occurs, or when we are engaged in extreme sports, for example.

This is a magical experience, and people will often attempt to recreate it through living on the edge, which can lead to very addictive or dangerous behavior. This "no time phenomenon" will occur over time with the practice of meditation. Seeing through the eyes of a child with a still mind will allow you to start with a clean slate where all things are possible. To a child, anything is possible until he's told it's not. In Zen Buddhism, this is called "beginner's mind."

Courting the Divine

Many spiritual seekers seek enlightenment in this world. Ironically, it's the seeking or attempting to obtain the spiritual that makes this realm so elusive. The path is always unfolding perfectly, and all the effort can become a silver cage. Setting the intention to evolve and surrendering to your soul's intention is a very powerful thing to do. The Eastern yin and yang principle of balance is an excellent analogy to convey this concept. The doing actually equates to resistance to allowing the divine energy of the universe to express itself through you. Thus, actively seeking creates an imbalance. It closes down our natural portal to the divine.

It's simply through being and taking action as an intuitive response that we are able to fulfill our greatest potential without attachment. This is the highest level of empowerment as a human being. The universe is always conspiring in our favor for us to fulfill our infinite potential.

The Non-Self

The compartmentalization created by the ego is complex and full of illusions. The illusions are created by the lack of knowing, and the mind fills in these knowledge gaps, creating its own reality. Just as mankind once thought that the earth was flat, so is the limited perspective that every man is an island. To believe that your thoughts and actions don't affect the rest of the planet is absurd once you experience the contrary. Once this is known, you could no more hurt another human being or creature than you could consciously hurt yourself. Hence the quote from Jesus, "Father, forgive them, for they do not know what they are doing" (Luke 23:34), when referring to his perpetrators.

This cannot be grasped with the limited perspective of the mind and can only be known through a direct realization via the infinite potentiality of the universe. Experiencing this melts all the internal facades that have always appeared to be so tangible, and allows the beauty and interconnectedness of all things to become visible. When this truth is not realized, people will adamantly defend their positions, for the truth threatens to dis-empower the ego. Therefore, it may be a futile effort to attempt to explain this concept to your mind. Self-lessness ultimately equates to death of the ego and the perception of separation.

Selfless Service

A mother once told me that if you want to have a spiritual experience have a child. But if it is enlightenment you seek, then have a difficult child. I laughed with her as we had a shared experience of being members of the same club, although I don't consider my child to be difficult. Being a parent who is present and emotionally available requires us to become selfless. Once all the resistance of trying to hold on to who you think you were subsides, you can see the magic that your love for this amazing little being allows in. It isn't necessary to have a child to go in the direction of selflessness. Being of service in your community or in an area that calls to you is great. Don't worry if your intentions are not purely selfless at first. Your consciousness will soon catch up to give you the gift that you weren't striving for.

Many people are so busy trying to get what they think they want only to find that what they wanted doesn't make them happy. So they continue seeking in this perpetual pattern expecting different results. Mother Teresa is one of many who demonstrated that she thoroughly understood that the gift is in the giving.

The Circle

With each new epiphany in life comes an expansion of consciousness and freedom from the rigid ego structures of the mind that are no longer appropriate. The infinite functions as a spherical, multidimensional process, as opposed to a linear one. Consequently, there are natural rhythms that occur as a result of things coming into balance. As the tide of the ocean surges and retracts, as we inhale and exhale, as we have a physical birth and death, so it is that nothing is ever lost. Energy changes and assumes a new form.

It is common to feel a contracted energy in your being after a new realization with a broadened awareness. This is because, with a new way of seeing, you suddenly become aware of the limitations of your psyche that have been in place but were unconscious. Suddenly, these limitations are conscious. In this process, it may feel like everything is going wrong, but the truth is that you have come to a place where you are now able to face what has already been there. Your mind simply needs to catch up. Of course, you can't *make* it happen. All you can do is stay in the now and accept what is. When there are no problems and only opportunities to make a decision that is when it will happen. The decision is to take action to implement a change or fully accept things the way they are. The charge on the situation is self-imposed by not doing one of these things. Therefore, one will create his or her own suffering by allowing subconscious belief systems to manifest, thus keeping with the status quo.

Believe It and You Will See It

The mind is a very powerful thing. It has the ability to fill in gaps of information and complete the picture that you are seeing or feeling automatically without a single conscious thought. This subconscious projection is a product of past experiences and belief systems of which you may not even be aware. Conversely, that which you are not open to, you will not experience. If you have a rigid idea of what life is supposed to look like, then that is what you will see. We are masters of our own being, and we have the ability to create our own reality. Here arises an opportunity to create your own gap consciously by disempowering the mind and creating a gap in time as we know it. By quieting the mind, we can enter a timeless space of infinite potentiality.

When we quiet the mind, we can choose to be open to what really is without instantaneously categorizing it and filling in the picture from a subconscious place. This is when the miracle happens, and we are present to experience it fully. The incessant, insane drive to be constantly distracted is ultimately based in the fear of cessation of our mere existence. Ironically, this is the very thing that keeps us dead. Hence, the saying by the Tibetan Buddhist: "Die before you die that you may truly live." The enlightened one sees things as they are and accepts being in the moment unconditionally.

Intention

Intention is the steering wheel for creating your reality. Setting your intention from a place of healthy non-attachment will allow you to utilize your infinite potential. What I mean by healthy non-attachment is staying out of the results. Ultimately, you are coming into alignment with your soul's intention, which is always patiently waiting to be revealed and expressed through you. As we are in the process of becoming more of ourselves, we don't have the complete picture yet because there is no complete picture. Try to wrap your finite mind around that one. This is where the knowing comes into play, which may be just beyond the mind's comprehension. And you know what? That's okay! Just like the song says ... *Let It Be.*

The Seed

The seed of your desire has been planted, and the universe is conspiring in your favor to help you manifest the pure substance of your soul in this realm. The subtle whisper in your ear that you don't always pay attention to or the idea that you may think is too grandiose for you to create is your soul's yearning to be fulfilled. Goethe said, "Whatever you can do or dream you can, begin it. Boldness has genius, power and magic in it. Begin it now." All of your needs will be met along the way. You don't need to wait until you have everything that you think you need in order to begin it. You already have the most powerful thing within you: your imagination. Modern science has proven the power of thought for living organisms. Studies have proven that prayer boosts the immune system to help people heal.

Creativity

We are all creative beings naturally. To what degree you can manifest and be in the flow of your creativity is dependent predominantly on your attachment to it. It can seem so illusive at times to see what dictates whether you are "in" or "out" of the flow. It can truly be miserable when you're "out" and are trying to get back "in." Therein lies the paradox because it just may not happen unless you allow it to. This can only be done by allowing Spirit to guide you through your greater potential. If you really like what you created or really dislike what you created, whether it's a poem or painting, it will put pressure on you to re-create or not to re-create the same thing.

The real gift is to place your attention on the process of creativity itself and then let it go from there. It will become whatever it will become. To place the attention on the end result and judge it will surely stifle your creativity. Being creative is one of life's great joys. If you think about the times in your life when you were truly present and felt very alive, you were creating. It is the process of creating itself that allows the natural joy that emanates from our soul to come forth. Being in love with the act of creativity will set you free in your creative expression.

Being Fully Present

I was listening to the Dalai Lama speak once, and he paused to take a drink of water. Time stopped as he drank the water. It was if nothing else in the world existed for those few seconds. His attention was completely focused on drinking the water. He was one with the water. The crowd was mesmerized at the intensity of his presence, and it became very quiet. What a gift it is to be able to be one hundred percent present in all that you do. You become available to experience the miracles that are always unfolding right before your eyes, the gift of life happening. It is all beautiful!

The Surface Mind

We all have a tendency to believe that the stream of incessant thought patterns that flow through the mind makes up who we are. This is simply not true. Discipline is the key, by quieting the mind and bringing your attention inward.

What does it take to wake up out of the mediocrity of the status quo and ignite your soul's passion? Listen. Listen to the big dream, the dream that has unlimited possibilities. Imagine and keep your feet moving. You will always receive exactly what you need on time and in time. Strangely enough, though, the information you receive will not be limited to the time-space continuum.

Aligning with Your Soul's Desire

In a recent group meeting, I found myself tapping into people's souls' desires. I had connected several people with loved ones who had passed and was feeling quite comfortable within the room. I found myself going deeper with the gentleman next to me. A voice was coming through me that was reaching down into him and unveiling his life's purpose. He was to focus on bringing joy to people in any way, shape, and form that he could. The voice was telling him to step out of who he thought he was and bring himself into alignment with the pure joy that was yearning to be expressed through him. I felt one hundred percent sure that this was his sole mission in life.

My attention then shifted to a woman. Her soul's desire was love and healing. The more she was able to give and share these qualities, the happier she would be. She was a natural healer and, as it turns out, she taught piano to children. She confessed that she was happiest when she touched these children on a deep level far beyond the piano lesson. I felt she had a belief that inhibited her from sharing this gift with adults. I reminded her that her gift was for all to receive.

Out of a group of ten people, I only knew the person who had invited me to speak. During a conversation at the end of the meeting, people began to share their occupations. The first gentleman just happened to be a comedy writer. He admitted that he loved to bring joy to people and wished he could do it all the time.

"You can!" I exclaimed. "You don't need to wait until you think that you have arrived at some enlightened place that your mind has conjured up. Simply side-step out of your identity and place your attention on expressing your gifts any way you can."

Stepping Outside of Your Identity

There is a prevalent belief in our society that we need to work things out before we can move on to the next level of spiritual maturity. What if you were able to take a lateral step and align yourself with your higher self? What if you were able to simply step outside of your identity and step into your infinite potential or your soul's greatest boundless expression, and live from that place?

The mind is a valuable tool, but it is also a trap. It can keep you very busy trying to work out all the endless facets of core problems that are manifesting unwanted patterns in your life. This is not a suggestion to be in denial of what needs to be understood. It is possible to have a collateral expansion of consciousness beyond the sole identification and limited idea of the ego. We do this by becoming less interested in the complexity of the mind's idea of itself and shifting our attention to that place where we are free. Free to use our imagination to explore what it is to be fully in the moment, experiencing the vastness of the universe internally as well as externally. This is not something to learn. This comes with the human operational manual, but we learn to forget. Take a look at a child deeply immersed in a creative process while his imagination is fully engaged navigating through realms, visions, dimensions and infinite ideas effortlessly.

Use the brilliance of your imagination and explore where you can go and what you can do when there are no limitations. If you're not having fun doing it, then your mind may be involved. We are supposed to have fun while engaged in this co-creative process of universal expression! Imagination is the root of all creativity. We are creative beings, and active practice of creating ignites our passion, vitality and energy to create more. It sets you free!

By attuning yourself with the qualities that your soul desires to express, you will be free to love unconditionally, and experience the love and joy of being for which there is no equal. As a pure expression of the perfection that you are, beyond identification with ego, you will constantly be opening up to new opportunities to share your unique gifts with the world. This is the ultimate expression of the liberation of the soul!

The Birth of Human Consciousness

Evolution of consciousness is non-linear, contrary to what the mind would have us believe. Permeated throughout many cultures, especially western, is an underlying idea that more is better. We believe that things or external circumstances will finally quench our thirst for happiness, and when we achieve them we will, once and for all, be able to relax. Since the beginning of time, man has been seeking a myriad of paths, techniques, etc., to find peace.

Many enlightened beings have shared their journey in hopes of helping others, but this is often misconstrued and taken literally instead of an example of one person's experience of stepping into their greater potential. This is analogous to thinking that something horrible is happening to a woman giving birth if you had no knowledge of the process.

Like childbirth, the birthing of human consciousness may seem painful at times, especially when one is externally focused. This creates a sense of separation and breeds more grasping and desperation, which often lead to more multi-tasking, distracting one further from being still. Greater multitasking creates more chaos in the mind and, consequently, the body. When there is harmony in the mind, there is harmony in the body, and vice versa. It's not that you can't do more, but it's like trying to spread the same amount of water over a greater surface area. It may still cover the area, but it is shallow.

And so it is with consciousness. Focusing completely on one thing at a time brings much greater depth to the experience. Immersed in the moment, with single-minded attention, you'll open the floodgates to fully experience the love, peace and joy that are your natural birthright.

Love

Love has no beginning and no end
Love cannot be contained, categorized or restricted
Love is the life force that is the universe
Love brings us home

—Daniel Ryan

Chapter 22

The Power of Prayer

Beyond the veil of duality, there is only love.
I will meet you there.

—*Daniel Ryan*

Communion with the one power, the one presence of the universe, is sacred. The capacity to connect and attune ourselves with the infinite intelligence of the one true Source is such a gift! The life force that dwells within is the impetus for this divine intelligence to express itself through our creativity and imagination. How we tap into and align ourselves with this one Source is our free will. How large of an expression of this innate life force and magnificent power of manifestation do you want to be? It is beyond the comprehension of our finite mind in this incarnation to see the magnitude of our vast potential to bring forth and be a vehicle for the one Source.

I find the theoretical idea of "free will" interesting. Of course, we have "free will" in the sense that we decide when or how to use this precious incarnation, but an interesting thing happens as we attune ourselves with the one power, the one Source, the one intelligence. Our will is the will of the innate intelligence or God of the universe desiring to co-create and express itself, through you and as you. This notion may sound foreign as the current state of race consciousness is still well-versed in a sense of separation and limitation.

This is the age of awakening, where this idea of lack and limitation has run its course. A vibration of higher consciousness is being ushered into this dimension, and the old paradigm no longer fits. The higher vibration that is currently being birthed on the planet is disintegrating the old myopic vision of our innate potential of God through and as us. The belief that God or the universe is separate from us—and that we are not accountable for the degree that we allow this Universal Intelligence to come forth through and as us—are becoming archaic.

The resolve of the empirical evidence through science is congruent with faith and the manifestation of prayer. Through this awakening, it is not such a different idea of what we have known, but simply a grander idea of the same, without the limitations. Throughout the ages, there have been clear signs to guide humankind to the full realization of self, beckoning emancipation from a limited idea of the self.

The answer lies in that small, still voice within that is guiding us very patiently and gracefully through the path of awakening. The question is answered in prayer, in meditation, in the awe of the miracle of the magnificence of life force present everywhere. Surrender is the key to opening the door from the small idea of "free will" and a rigid, archaic paradigm to an infinite and exciting vision of that which we are capable of doing. There was a time when man thought it was impossible to fly—until the Wright brothers had a vision that they implemented through action. There was a time when man thought it was impossible to travel to the moon—until the vision was birthed through action. And so it is as we step into a new vision of our vast potential, manifesting from the one Source, that we tap into the realization of oneness, where authentic freedom lies.

Prayer

The whisper of the eternal making it all clear
A time to remember that we are so very dear
The infinite well of kindness that fills our cup
Communion with our beloved, time is never up
Love beyond borders, love beyond fear
Inclusive compassion we need not compare
How good it is being aware of our answered prayer

—Daniel Ryan

Chapter 23

Earth-Shaking Epiphany

Each morning, we are born again.
What we do today is what matters most.

—Buddha

This book may be at an end, but your journey is just beginning. If you're feeling a little overwhelmed by all that you have read, rest assured that we are all on this spiritual path together. Along with you, I am still learning to read the signs along the way, as the following humorous story reveals . . .

I was jostled from a deep sleep by an energetic vibration throughout my body. Excited by the prospect of divine spiritual intervention, I took notice. Was this the moment that I had been waiting for in my non-grasping practice of striving not to strive? Had my years of inward contemplation, non-judgmental observation, healthy detachment, dis-identification with the mind, equanimity across all paradigms, and being completely immersed in the moment finally paid off? Was this my moment of emancipation from the confines of the rigid compartmentalization of the ego's prison?

The vibration intensified. Now it seemed as if the whole bed was shaking. I wanted to wake my wife and have her share in this state of exaltation. Excitement flooded my being, and I wanted to shout from the mountaintops, "I'm free!" No longer would I have to swim through the murky waters of projections born of stagnant intracellular memories of present and past life experiences.

The vibration now became an actual thumping. Wow, Spirit is really trying to send me a message, I thought. Okay, I'm all ears. Yes, Spirit, I'm available to become the flow of the universe. Yes, Spirit, use me. Thy will be done on earth as it is in heaven. Yes, heaven is right here, right now, and I say yes to the recognition of the realization of oneness. Yes, God, almighty spirit, Universal Intelligence, the one Source, I'm ready to be used as a divine vehicle and inspiration for all to partake and bear witness to. I know that this transformation will allow others to come forward and embrace their own divinity, magnificence and beauty.

Slowly but enthusiastically, I opened my eyes to see how my perception had changed from this earth-shaking experience. The ceiling looked the same, but the bed was still shaking with an intense thumping. I allowed my gaze to fall toward my feet. Lo and behold, my eight-and-a-half-pound Papillion puppy was sprawled out on his back. Deep in a dream, his little body was simulating what appeared to be running and playing.

Hmmmm, so much for earth-shaking epiphanies . . .

Acknowledgments

The guidance of the many messengers of spirit that have influenced my journey, my brothers and sisters and extended family, Jack and Sue Giauque for all of your support and insightful notes. Ginny Weissman for all the amazing guidance, and Paul Burt, my publishers, for believing in the vision. Debbie, Eric, Mari, Ellie, Susan, Chris, Michael, Nora, Monique, Nikki, Olga, Lisa, Helene, Trish, Ellen, Andrea, Richard, Roxanne, Anne, Josh, Evan, Fredrick, Amber, Jakki, Jennifer, Jeff, Margie, Roger, Laurie, Kristen, Kate, Kit, Mimo, Michelle, Sonia, Stephen, Tiffany, Wendi, Jave, Anya, Camille, Christie, Laurie, Yoka, Steven, Tommy, Sundari, Cynthia, Kathy, Laurie, Lorelei, Shannon, Patrice, Janet, and all the Angels that hold the presence at the healing circles. Alan Zweibel, brilliant editing of Susan Heim, Mark DeCarlo, Chris Paine, Randy Rogers, Liz Sanders, Dr. James Peace, Patrick Leonard, Judy Nadler, Mark Chambers, Nita Vallens and MB. And finally thank you to all those that have permitted me to share your stories.

About the Author

DR. DANIEL RYAN, D.C., a dynamic healer, mystic, and spiritual medium, has transformed numerous lives while also enjoying a separate and successful private Chiropractic practice since 1988. He has been referred to as "Doctor to the Stars" on the Lifetime Channel and recognized as one of the "Top Doctors" on Southern California's KCAL TV. He is internationally known for his many appearances and workshops where he teaches meditation and acts as a conduit for spiritual communication and transdimensional healing.

Dr. Ryan holds a Bachelor of Science degree in Human Biology and Doctorate degree in Chiropractic as well. But this book is not about chiropractic or his work as a chiropractor. Instead, this book is devoted to his education, experience, and teaching in the fields of spiritual and energetic healing and liberation.

Dr. Ryan currently resides in Southern California with his amazing wife, two creative and courageous daughters and Papillion dog.

www.healingfromheavenbook.com

Transformation Media Books

Transformation Media Books is dedicated to publishing innovative works that nourish the body, mind and spirit, written by authors whose ideas and messages make a difference in the world.

Please visit our website:

www.TransformationMediaBooks.com
For more information, the latest titles or to purchase direct

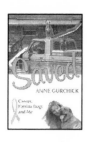

Saved
Cancer, Katrina Dogs and Me

Anne Gurchick

ISBN: 978-0-9852737-2-9
$16.95

Despite her own health challenges, Anne Gurchick follows her passion for animals to Hurricane Katrina devastated New Orleans. Saved through her selfless efforts, Anne finds strength and healing in rescuing stranded dogs. Connect with Anne and her friends on a heartbreaking and heartwarming journey. A true story you won't soon forget.

"If you look up the word hope in the dictionary you might just see Anne Gurchick's picture there. In the middle of her own battle with cancer she reaches out to save some of the most forgotten and battered victims of Hurricane Katrina. Anne's story is cause for celebration and the parallels between her journey to wellness and reaching out to the 'four leggeds' is further proof that we are inextricably connected to our animals and if we choose to listen, the lessons they give us can change our lives."

—John St.Augustine
Radio Host and Author
Every Moment Matters

"Anne's book, *Saved,* is an honest account of the power of purpose and commitment, as an antidote to fear and loss. Anne walks through her deepest fears and discovers hope, humor and unconditional love amidst immense devastation. Allow yourself to be inspired and to enjoy her wonderful journey!"

—Annie Denver, MA
Aspen, CO

Sooner or Later
Restoring Sanity to Your End-of-Life Care

Damiano deSano Iocovozzi MSN FNP CNS

ISBN: 978-0-9842258-6-6
Retail List: $12.95 USD

Sooner or Later offers patient, family and caregivers a safe place to help process turbulent emotions during the diagnosis phase of a serious or terminal illness and remain sane, rational and in control.

Sooner or Later provides the information and tools to empower patients and their families to seek the appropriate level of care, take control and make good decisions to maintain the best quality of life.

"*Sooner or Later* is a rare treasure. This book shines with compassion, wisdom, humor, and truth. I believe it should be must reading for everyone. Really!"

—Christiane Northrup, M.D. ob/gyn physician
and author of the *New York Times* bestsellers:
Women's Bodies, Women's Wisdom and *The Wisdom of Menopause*

Don't Die without Me! is the eBook version of
Sooner or Later

New eBook available at Amazon, BarnesandNoble.com, and other fine retailers including
http://www.smashwords.com/books/view/105018

Don't Die Without Me! provides the pertinent questions to ask medical specialists written in a way the reader and provider understand.

Don't Go to the Doctor without Me!
Damiano deSano Iocovozzi MSN FNP CNS

New eBook available at Amazon, BarnesandNoble.com, and other fine retailers including
http://www.smashwords.com/books/view/95147

Don't Go to the Doctor without Me! is your personal road map through the health care maze from wellness exams to chronic care management, teaching you how to be your own health care advocate. Uninsured or under insured, this book includes important tips on how to get low cost or free services while still receiving the best possible care. All the questions patients should ask.

Sereni-Tea
Sipping Self Success

Dharlene Marie Fahl

ISBN: 978-0-9844600-3-8
Retail List Prices: $15.95 USD,
$17.00 CAD, £ 12.95 GBP

Certified tea specialist, Dharlene Marie Fahl, guides you on an inner journey of self-discovery through the simple practice of sipping tea. Quiet your mind, open your heart and nurture your being as you drink in the peace of self success. Anywhere, anytime, your cup of Sereni-Tea awaits you.

> "*Sereni-Tea* is not a typical book about tea. Yes, it contains all the necessary information to help both novices and experts alike to better appreciate this near-miraculous beverage, but then it uses tea as a means for discovering who we are and what we could become . . ."
> —Joe Simrany, President, Tea Association of the USA

Dying for a Change

William L. Murtha

ISBN: 978-0-9823850-8-1
Retail List: $19.95 USD

Dying for a Change is the gripping, true account of William L. Murtha's fight to survive hypothermia in the freezing waters off the coast of Britain. At a crucial time when his life was rapidly spiraling out of control, William was swept out to sea by a twenty-foot freak wave. Drowning, losing consciousness and convinced that this was the end, he relived many pivotal moments from his past and experienced a life-changing conversation with a Higher Presence.

William's compelling message inspires readers to come face-to-face with their own deepest fears and challenges perceptions about God, life, death and miracles.

> "An amazing story! . . . takes away any doubt that there is an energy force out there ready to help us find our way . . . we need only listen."
> —Susan Jeffers, Ph.D, Author, *Feel the Fear and Do It Anyway*®

The Key of Life
A Metaphysical Investigation

Randolph J. Rogers

ISBN: 978-0-9823850-9-8
Retail List: $18.95 USD

Newsman Randy Rogers takes you along on his riveting journey investigating past lives, present events and reincarnation. Randy proves that "ordinary" people can experience the extraordinary when they open themselves to the possibilities.

The Key of Life is a true story about who we are, why we are here and how we are all connected.

". . . a consciousness-raising self-help detective story . . ."
—Peter Michalos, Author of *Psyche, a Novel of the Young Freud*

". . . a very personal and life changing experience . . . We emerge from it . . . enlightened, inspired."
—Maria Shriver, First Lady of California, Author

EAT IT UP!
The Complete Mind/Body/Spirit Guide to a Full Life After Weight Loss Surgery

Connie Stapleton, Ph. D.

ISBN: 978-0-9823850-7-4
Retail List: $15.95 USD

Eat It Up! is the first book incorporating a whole person, mind/body/spirit approach to prevent weight regain in the months and years following weight loss surgery. Written with humor, compassion and a "firm and fair" approach, *Eat It Up!* is a must-have for the millions who are obese or overweight.

"*Eat It Up!* is a must-have book for surgical weight loss patients. Dr. Stapleton goes beyond the "how to" of maintaining weight loss following surgery to providing skills, wisdom and the support necessary to create a fully healthy and balanced life."
—John C. Friel, Ph.D., Licensed Psychologist,
New York Times best-selling author

Tragedy in Sedona
My Life in James Arthur Ray's Inner Circle

Connie Joy

ISBN: 978-0-9845751-6-9
Retail List: $18.95 USD

Follow Connie Joy inside the seminars and once-in-a-lifetime trips to Egypt and Peru for an up close look at the transformative work of a charismatic teacher—and the underlying danger of mixing up the message with the messenger!

Connie and her husband attended 27 events over three years presented by James Arthur Ray, "Rock Star of Personal Transformation." In 2007, Connie participated in Ray's sweat lodge, a Native American ceremonial sauna meant to be a place of spiritual renewal and mental and physical healing. In reality it was just a test of human endurance for Connie and the other participants. Her prediction that someone could be seriously hurt came true in October 2009 when three people died and 18 participants were injured during a sweat lodge run by James Arthur Ray and his staff.

After injuries at his previous events, why didn't Ray get the message he was literally playing with fire?

After a four month trial, Ray was convicted of three counts of negligent homicide and began serving two years in prison in November, 2011 on each count concurrently. He also is facing a wrongful death suit for the suicide of Colleen Conaway at one of his seminars ten weeks prior to the sweat lodge deaths.

"James Ray's debut in the film, *The Secret,* thrust him into the spotlight . . . appearances on *Oprah* and *Larry King Live* . . . *Tragedy in Sedona* is a behind the scenes look at the rise and fall of the James Ray Empire, through the eyes of an ultimately disenchanted follower. Connie Joy takes you on her personal and authentic journey—from being a devoted member of James' inner circle and Dream Team to . . . trying to warn others."

—From the Foreword by forensic
psychiatrist Dr. Carole Lieberman

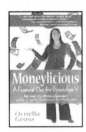

Moneylicious
  A Financial Clue for Generation Y

Ornella Grosz

ISBN: 978-0-9845751-1-4
Retail List: $12.95 USD

Spend and invest your hard-earned dollars in an effective way! Moneylicious is an easy-to-understand guide for Gen Y and everyone needing to understand how money and personal finance work. Twenty-something Ornella Grosz will help you recover, or better yet avoid, the slippery slope of debt!

Moneylicious: A Financial Clue for Generation Y explains the basis of investing, banking, purchasing a first home, the importance of spending with a touch of humor (yes, you can buy that $100 pair of jeans). And much more!

"For Gen Y . . . written by Gen Y . . . *Moneylicious* provides a great financial roadmap. Ornella's willingness to share her own stories not only engages the reader but creates a learning environment where the basics of money and investing are not only explained . . . but shared in a way that is entertaining as well as experiential. This book should be required reading for all young people in high school and college. Armed with the knowledge that Ornella shares, the readers will be prepared to not only survive . . . but to thrive in the financial world they face."

—Sharon Lechter, Founder and CEO of Pay Your Family First,
member of the first President's Advisory Council
on Financial Literacy, the AICPA Financial Literacy
Commission and co-author of the National Bestseller
Think and Grow Rich—Three Feet From Gold

Shift Happens!
Reinvent Yourself Using Innovative Solutions

James D. Feldman

ISBN: 978-0-9846359-4-8
Retail List: $15.95 USD
New eBook available at Amazon, BarnesandNoble.com,
and other fine retailers including
http://www.smashwords.com/books/view/60296

When Shift Happens you can manage it or let it manage you. Succeeding after shifts in his own life, Feldman illustrates how to stop limiting yourself, retake control and immediately start using change to your advantage. Want to break free of the past, boost your energy, and impact the future? Learn how to apply 3D Thinking to discover innovative solutions in times of high velocity change.

"Turbulence is inevitable, misery is optional. I learned that the hard way, taking Braniff International successfully through financial crisis. Jim Feldman lays out a great flight plan for you to fly through turbulence and not only survive, but thrive. He shares his own turbulent experiences as well as real life experiences of others."

Howard Putnam, Former CEO,
Southwest Airlines and Braniff International Airways,
Speaker and Author of *The Winds of Turbulence*

"Shift Happens to everyone. Make yours positive now and read my friend James' insightful book."

Mark Victor Hansen, Co-founder,
Chicken Soup for the Soul Series

"Jim Feldman is a genius on marketing and positioning. This book is chock full of ideas that can move you onwards and upwards in business and in life."

Dr. Nido Qubein, President, High Point University
Chairman, Great Harvest Bread Co.

CPSIA information can be obtained at www.ICGtesting.com
Printed in the USA
BVOW070428280613

324558BV00001B/4/P